God Made the Aliens

Making Sense of Extraterrestrial Contact

Table of Contents

Chapter One: Someone Happened
Real Visitations
Astonishing Civilizations
Defining the "Gods"

Chapter Two: A World of Contact
Our Origins
Water Worlds
Globetrotters?

Chapter Three: Too Strange for Fiction
A Combustible Relationship
Strength in Numbers
Dark Forces
They Might be Giants

Chapter Four: The Angel-Alien Connection
A *Crick* Word about the Origin of Life
Physical Beings
UFAs: Unidentified Flying Angels
Angelic Abductions
Alone in the Universe?

Chapter Five: God Made the Aliens
God of All
A Book like no other
That Kind of Creator
The Ultimate Extraterrestrial
God Made the Aliens

Preface

I will keep this introduction brief, because we have a lot of interesting topics to cover! My purpose in writing this book is to provide a guide for grappling with an issue that I feel is extremely underdeveloped in Christian thinking: extraterrestrials. Within this primary issue, many others arise that are also ignored. Among them are UFOs, giants, demonic possession, spontaneous human combustion, and a host of others. In fact, these topics are not only avoided, but are even thought to be completely taboo. After much investigation, I have become convinced that extraterrestrials exist, and that there is at least a grain of truth to all of these matters. I hope to prove this point throughout the book. Of course—and as it always seems to be—the reality of these issues may actually point us in a direction we never expected to travel. On the one hand, extraterrestrial contact is more mysterious and complex than you or I ever imagined. On the other hand, it has been staring us in the face for eons.

   This book is not only a guide, but also a call to awareness. It is time for the church, and believers everywhere, to quit ignoring or impugning the existence of extraterrestrials, and to begin an honest inquiry into these beings. I am emphatic about this for two major reasons. The first is that, if extraterrestrials are a part of our reality, they are also a part of our search for truth. As Jesus so famously said, the truth—that is, any and all truth—really will "set you free." The second reason is that the existence of beings other than ourselves would also bolster our faith, and further confirm the biblical metanarrative. Far from being evidence against the existence of God or biblical teachings, extraterrestrial contact can actually provide very formidable reasons to accept both. But a word of caution from the start: what I mean by "extraterrestrial" will probably turn out to be a lot different than what you are currently thinking. I will not spoil this twist now, but it will no doubt become apparent as you continue reading.

While the contents of this book should be interesting to absolutely anyone who wonders whether or not we are alone in our existence, I distinctly wish to help people of faith to make sense of these matters. That is not to say that nonbelievers should close this book, and ignore the topics I will be addressing. In fact, I provide what I feel are *very* powerful reasons why an atheist or an agnostic should question their worldviews, and perhaps at least entertain the idea that we are not the only intelligent beings in existence. It's just that my specific goal is to reconcile these topics from a position of religious faith. What follows is one Christian's investigation into something that truly can change the way we view almost every aspect of life. I hope you will find more than a few items that cause you to really think, to really ponder, and to really change the way you view our place in God's Creation.

Chapter One

Someone Happened

When I was about nine years old, I saw the most incredible thing. While camping with my family near the western basin of Lake Erie, we all sat mesmerized for the better part of an entire night. On a relatively cool, overcast summer evening, some type of machine hovered in the air. The moon itself was scarcely visible that night because of the clouds, but the craft certainly was. We all saw it: my brother, my father, my mother, and I. Given how long ago this happened, it is difficult to recall how large it was, or how high it floated in the air. All I remember is seeing multiple lights, a dome-shaped body, and thinking one thing to myself—what type of object can literally sit still in the air? Have you ever seen an aircraft that remained perfectly fixed in the sky for hours on end? I knew of no object that could do that, much less any craft that could. I still don't.

I'm sure this sounds a bit familiar to some readers. Sure, a "dome-shaped" object with lights around it. How typical. How cliché. Cliché or not, that is what we saw. Since that time, I have seen a number of things in the sky that I thought were odd, but nothing that I feel very strongly was not man-made. When I decided to go into the field of biblical studies as young man, I came to have mixed feelings about our sighting, and the overall topic of UFOs. My first response was to dismiss every last bit of it as the musings of people who were either insane, or were simply starved for attention. I also dismissed our sighting as being nothing unusual. There couldn't really be anything to this stuff, right?

But as I actually began to really research the beliefs and traditions of the earliest cultures—some of which I share in this book—it started to become obvious that I could not so easily dismiss these ideas. There certainly seems to be something to it: at least *something*. So, how could I reconcile the strange sightings and stories about unexplained spacecraft and unknown entities? How could the legends of "visitations," and the almost unanimous view that other beings played a role in our earliest civilizations, be in any way squared with what I believed as a Christian?

I believe the answer is very surprising, but also deceptively obvious. All of this became easier to put together when I began to read the Bible in a more straightforward fashion. When one ceases to view the Bible in some overly philosophical way—as I admittedly did for many years—they tend to finally see the text for what it is: for what the original authors really intended it to be. You start to understand their experiences the way they actually did. Maybe when they saw beings "come down" from the sky, they were *really* seeing beings come down from the sky. Maybe when they talked about seeing "spinning wheels" or unknown "chariots," they were *really* seeing those things. Maybe—just maybe—there is a parallel between the angels depicted within the Bible and the extraterrestrials described by so many other people and ancient traditions.

More than any of this, perhaps all of these ideas can work together to further prove the beliefs that both Jews and Christians hold sacred. I had to find out if this were so. What follows is my research into these issues, and the conclusions that have come from it. I invite you to read, reflect, question, and honestly consider what I have found. Whether you end up agreeing with me or not, I guarantee you will be challenged to come to terms with your own view on these matters.

I want to begin this effort by actually showing you that strange and unexplainable things really do happen. There are an amazing number of air sightings, unbelievably advanced ancient architecture, and frankly, impossible connections that existed between cultures that could not have been physically associated with one another. There are also occurrences that happen in this world that are downright bizarre in nature: things stranger than fiction, so to speak. There is a great abundance of sources where one can read about these realities, so my attempt here is not to catalog everything I can think of. Instead, I just want to provide some really good information that should at least get you to the place where I first began: to the point where you have to say, "maybe I can't just completely dismiss all of this." If you can arrive at that place in your thinking, you may just be willing to venture the rest of the way with me.

Real Visitations

It was December 9, 1965, when thousands of people living in both Canada and the United States reported seeing an incredibly strange flying object traveling through the night skies. The blazing object was rumored to have left a rather noticeable amount of metal debris in its path, before finally ending up in Kecksburg, Pennsylvania.[1] Surely, this was simply a military experiment, a meteorite, or something of the sort. They always are. But the folks in Kecksburg certainly don't believe that to be the case; they take pride in "Pennsylvania's Roswell" incident. To this day, the Kecksburg UFO Festival commemorates the unexplained sighting. That's quite a tradition, for something that obviously "never happened."

A more impressive event occurred roughly a decade prior, this time across the globe in Florence, Italy. A 2014 BBC news article revisited this astonishing incident, calling it "The day UFOs stopped play."[2] This strange happening was not seen by just a few witnesses, or even hundreds. This was an experience shared by many *thousands* of ardent sports fans that day. Concerning this sighting, the article records the following:

> "Ten-thousand fans were watching in the concrete bowl of the Stadio Artemi Franchi. But just after half-time the stadium fell eerily silent - then a roar went up from the crowd. The spectators were no longer watching the match,

---

[1] C. David, "The most legit UFO sightings."
[2] Richard Padula, "The day UFOs stopped play."

but were looking up at the sky, fingers pointing. The players stopped playing, the ball rolled to a stand-still."³

With so many people having witnessed the event, there are naturally different descriptions of what was seen that day. There seem to have been multiple types of crafts, some said to resemble "Cuban cigars" moving about in the air, and others looking more egg-like.

But perhaps this was simply a matter of a few people within the crowd whipping everyone into a frenzy. The article flattens such a notion, saying, "The incident at the stadium cannot simply be interpreted as mass hysteria - there were numerous UFO sightings in many towns across Tuscany that day and over the days that followed."⁴ Again, everyone in the stadium witnessed this event. Even the players stopped to observe these phenomena! Nearly all of the articles about this mentioned the reported presence of a sticky "angel hair" or glittery substance that fell from the sky around the stadium. A chemical analysis of this material revealed traces of boron, silicon, calcium, and magnesium.⁵ But no one could tell what it really was. One of the more noted explanations for both the cigar-shaped objects and the sticky substance was migrating spiders, as they linked their webs together during travel.⁶ I'm not joking. There still haven't been any remotely reasonable naturalistic explanations offered to solve the mystery.

Then there is the case of the enigmatic "V-shaped lights" seen by a great many spectators in the Hudson Valley area, on the night of March 24th, 1983. While UFO sightings have been very pronounced in this part of the country over the last century, more than three hundred people actually called to report this particular occurrence. It is unknown how many others saw the event, but did not choose to report it. Most described seeing a ". . . large V-shaped array of lights that

---

³ Ibid.
⁴ Ibid.
⁵ See McClellan's article, "Spiders blamed for mass UFO sighting."
⁶ Ibid.

moved slowly and almost silently through the sky."[7] This V-shaped pattern of lights has been a trademark of many other unidentified sightings.[8]

One of the most significant U.S. sightings, which simply must be mentioned, occurred at Chicago's O'Hare International Airport. On November 7, 2006, a host of individuals saw a metallic object hovering above Gate C-17 that simply should not have been there. As with any such sighting, there are some questions about just how many people saw the craft, and precisely what it looked like. There is a consensus, however, on its activity. Jon Hilkevitch, of the *Chicago Tribune*, summarized this in the following way: "All agreed the object made no noise and it was at a fixed position in the sky, just below the 1,900-foot cloud deck, until shooting off into the clouds."[9] We also know that an entire group of airline employees saw this object, as well as various others from around the location. Airline employees tend to make very poor liars in these situations, since their jobs could very well depend on what they have to say. The FAA (Federal Aviation Administration) decided not to launch a full-scale investigation into the matter, concluding that it was just some type of weather phenomenon. Go figure.

It is important to note that we need to be careful whenever we speak about "UFOs" (unidentified flying objects), or the newer form, "UAPs" (unidentified aerial phenomena); we need to tread lightly. Simply not knowing exactly what an object is does not mean it is an alien spacecraft. Rather, it only means it is unidentified. It could be a man-made craft, or any number of natural phenomena. Most are, actually. It would be completely rash to start attributing every strange sight to the workings of extraterrestrials. However, it would be equally rash to ignore the *small* (but very real) percentage of events and sightings that most definitely

---

[7] See Kiger's article, "Top 10 Mass Sightings of UFOs."
[8] For example, the very same description was given by the *thousands* of people throughout Nevada and Arizona who witnessed the so-called "Phoenix Lights" on the night of March 13, 1997. Ibid.
[9] See Hilkevitch's article, "In the sky! A bird? A plane? A . . . UFO?"

point in that direction. If even one—just one—of these events is the product of beings who exist somewhere beyond Earth, then it would prove that they exist. Think about that.

Typically, even those who have spent a tremendous amount of time studying these bizarre sightings are quite cautious in their approach. This is not only understandable, but is actually extremely good for the entire enterprise. We live at a time (still) where the prospect of reporting an unexplainable craft leaves one open to mockery, harassment, or even to career termination. The more "sightings" that really can be explained as either man-made or natural phenomena, the less credence anyone has in reporting things that cannot be explained as such. In other words, it becomes harder to report on unexplained activities if they increasingly appear to be either fictitious or explainable.

In her very robust book on UFOs—called, *UFOs: Generals, Pilots, and Government Officials Go on the Record*—Leslie Kean (and associates) detailed the kind of fear that exists among flight professionals: professionals who are afraid they might lose their jobs, simply for suggesting that they saw an odd craft in the sky. These are the kinds of people who we rely upon to fly our commercial liners, operate our military aircrafts, and even command our military operations.

For a variety of reasons that are discussed within the book, the U.S. government has seemed to suppress the voices of those who experienced unexplainable crafts. Concerning the U.S. and its efforts (or lack thereof) in properly studying UFOs, Kean offers the following:

> "In the early 1950s, it established Project Blue Book, a small agency that received reports from citizens, investigated the reports, and offered explanations to the media and the public. Blue Book gradually solidified as largely a public relations effort intent on debunking UFO sightings. Hundreds of files accumulated, and the Air Force closed down the program in 1970, ending all official investigations—or so they said

publicly—without having found an explanation for many shocking UFO incidents . . . Our government still stays out of the UFO controversy and has no policy in place to address growing concern."[10]

One can only imagine how much more we might know about UFOs in this country, if our government had ever really taken any genuine interest in the issue. Worse, maybe they have taken interest, and have suppressed the information. Scores of people believe that to be the case.

Not only does Kean's book show how stifled the issue of UFOs has been—in the U.S. especially—it also displays countless authorities who took the chance to speak out anyway. Without question, one of the more impressive examples of this is Dr. Richard Haines, who is a former senior research scientist with NASA. In his time there, he came across scores of cases where UFOs (UAPs, as he termed them) had been seen. As a result, he compiled a detailed report titled, "Aviation Safety in America—A Previously Neglected Factor."[11] As Kean pointed out, the "neglected factor" was UAP sightings. In this report, Haines recorded *more than 100 cases* where pilots had encountered these objects, with six of those being "near misses," in which the UAP evaded the pilot's craft at the last moment. That seems to be a common theme in these instances.

In addition to these findings, Haines went on to set up an international database that contained more than 3,400 firsthand cases of UAP sightings. This database, combined with the slew of professionally trained pilots who attested to having sightings, should really give us pause. Dr. Haines is not the type of person we are used to hearing from on this issue. Based on his former position at NASA, he risked both his own credibility and the potential for all variety of other repercussions in

---

[10] Leslie Kean, *UFOs*, 9.
[11] Ibid. 42

disclosing this information. He is about as trustworthy a source as we could imagine. But he is not the only one.

Among the plethora of other significant people Kean mentions, Neil Daniels also comes to the forefront of this discussion. Daniels—a United Airlines Captain for thirty-five years—had an incredible sighting of his own during a flight from San Francisco to Boston Logan International Airport.[12] On that particular trip, he, his copilot, and a flight engineer, saw an intensely bright light moving about 1,000 yards away from their DC-10. While on autopilot, they were physically pulled towards this "light," which was then identified as some type of flying vehicle. Before they could make any real sense of what was happening, the craft blazed out of their sight at a speed that clearly surpassed the capabilities of anything man-made. Like many other pilots who have seen unexplainable things in the sky, he decided it was best to keep his mouth shut. But after seven months of contemplation, he opted to tell his boss what he had seen. The response was both typical and telling: "Bad things can happen to pilots who say they have these sightings."[13]

A little earlier, I mentioned that I had experienced a sighting of this variety when I was much younger. I realize that a personal testimony like my own—or something coming from "Farmer Joe" and his son, who saw a UFO in their back yard—is difficult to believe. It's not that such testimonies are not occasionally valid, but that they are very difficult to corroborate. Hopefully, you see that we do not simply have to trust these types of accounts. Rather, there are also many credible accounts coming from massive crowds of people, all manner of military personnel, and those who pilot our commercial airliners.

We can be sure that most people who claim to see an unidentified flying object are not seeing an extraterrestrial craft, but we should also acknowledge that some people actually appear to be. While most accounts can be explained under closer investigation, there are a small number that

---

[12] Ibid. 45-46
[13] Ibid. 46

simply cannot: not even by our aeronautical experts. While these sightings—and *countless* others that have occurred—do suggest that there are other intelligent beings out there, UFOs are by no stretch the only indicator of that. We now come back down to Earth, so to speak, and examine a myriad of oddities from around the world. These will further illustrate that human beings have never been the only intelligent game in town.

Astonishing Civilizations

Very near to the time of the great Hudson Valley UFO sighting, a startled diver on the other side of the globe was busy discovering an incredibly elaborate underwater city off the coast of Japan. This site, often referred to as the "Yonaguni Pyramid," contains indications of advanced intelligent construction. While some have of course suggested that this grand structure is simply the result of natural processes, other scientists see a structure that is clearly a " . . . man-made monolith carved from a natural formation."[14] In my opinion, any person with eyes to see can tell that the Yonaguni Pyramid has the fingerprints of intelligence all over it. There are too many straight edges, perfect angles, and the like, to be the product of water erosion or other natural occurrences. Go ahead, "Google it" yourself. You be the judge.

    Other underwater buildings exist at various places around the globe, all containing their own mysterious and highly sophisticated architecture. While the Yonaguni Pyramid is still somewhat debated, no one doubts that the lost city of Pavlopetri ("Paul's stone") is a man-made complex. Discovered by Nicholas Flemming off the coast of Greece in 1967, Pavlopetri occupies about 20 acres of seabed, and is thought to have once contained as many as 4,000 people.[15] There is a large space in

---

[14] See The Faram Research Foundation's, "Yonaguni Pyramid."
[15] For more information, see *National Geographic's* series, "Drain the Oceans: Legends of Atlantis" (S5E1).

the middle of the ruined streets, perhaps where a market once stood, and also a large spot for a civic building or temple. Based on pottery found at the site, Pavlopetri was probably a fully functioning city from about 1100 BC to 1500 AD, when the civilization mysteriously came to a halt.[16] Now it all eerily rests beneath the ocean.

Though civilizations like these are sometimes considered to be more interesting than others because they are *now* below sea level—there is certainly a very mysterious aspect to them—they were not built underwater. Rather, they were constructed on land and covered with water later on. This occurred at different times, but some were covered perhaps as early as the end of the last ice age.[17] This by no means detracts from the peculiarity of their engineering. Instead, it shows us that such things were possible even for the oldest civilizations!

The oceans are of course not the primary places we find advanced ancient civilizations. Most are at least vaguely aware of innovative cultures like the Mayans and the Egyptians. To this day, both the Mayan understanding of astronomy and time and the ancient Egyptian understanding of engineering continue to baffle even the most educated professionals among us. I suspect this will always be the case.

During the "Classic Period" of the Mayan civilization—which roughly spanned 300-900 AD—they developed a very advanced understanding of astronomy.[18] During this time, they were able to predict solar eclipses, use astrological cycles for planting and harvesting crops, and even create two different calendars that are *as accurate as our own*.[19] All of this, more than one thousand years before us! Of course, they also developed extremely intricate temples, cities, and other architectural wonders, in addition to their unreasonable understanding of the surrounding cosmos.

---

[16] Ibid.
[17] Though the estimates for the exact timing of our last glacial period differ dramatically, it is commonly accepted that it ended somewhere near the 11th or 12th century BC.
[18] See *History's*, "Mayan Scientific Achievements."
[19] Ibid.

When we consider ancient architecture, most of us immediately think of the Egyptians, and that is warranted. The ancient Egyptians were able to construct what are still some of the most complex structures ever conceived by man. The Great Pyramid of Giza—the oldest of the Seven Wonders of the World—is the best-known example of such architecture. It still stands more than 450 feet high, and is comprised of an astonishing 2,300,000 blocks, each averaging about 2.5 tons in weight.[20] Not surprisingly, one of the central issues we have always faced in explaining the Great Pyramid is both the weight and number of these blocks. How did they strategically place so many massive blocks, particularly as the pyramid grew taller and taller? Perhaps equally complex is its three main chambers, all of which are full of complicated ventilation systems. Further, its walls are accurately oriented to match the four cardinal points of the compass.[21]

Even today, the exact method of construction eludes positive identification, but the Greek historian, Herodotus, claimed that it took nearly twenty years to construct and required a workforce of roughly 100,000 men.[22] Accurate or not, no one doubts that it was an astonishing undertaking for that day and age. It would be an astonishing undertaking in our day and age, for that matter. Modern archaeological and engineering groups from across the globe have attempted to move and assemble the types of massive stones used in the Great Pyramid—using all known ancient methods—to no avail. It's no wonder why, either. Not only would we need to hoist a plethora of 2-ton (plus or minus) blocks higher than 450 feet into the air (ultimately)—no one has found a suitable way they could have done that, to date—we would also have to ensure that the blocks properly fit with one another. That involves very precise cutting methods, and for each of those 2,300,000 blocks. Then there is the issue of creating intricate internal passages within the pyramid itself, so

---

[20] Lee Krystek, "Khufu's Great Pyramid."
[21] See "Pyramids of Giza" in the Encyclopaedia Britannica.
[22] Ibid.

that light could be seen into its deep chambers at particular times of the year. No big deal, right?

The age-old "single ramp theory"—whereby the Egyptians supposedly used a giant ramp, in order to slide the blocks—has been clearly refuted, if nothing else because the ramp would end up being larger than the pyramid itself. The shape of the ramp would resemble a door stop: a very large doorstop. As the pyramid grew in height, the size of the ramp would have to increase with it, meaning that the ramp would slowly become longer and longer. In fact, the ramp would have to be about one mile in length in order to have accomplished its task.[23] As the pyramid grew towards its completion, the ramp would end up being an achievement equal to (or even surpassing) the pyramid itself. We would have to add the ramp as another incredible piece of architecture! Of course, pulling countless 2-ton bricks on an uphill ramp for the distance of a mile is, well, difficult to imagine in its own right.

It has also been offered that the pyramids were constructed by spiral ramps, which allowed builders to pull the bricks along the exterior of the pyramid. Besides the fact that pulling blocks of that size consistently up a ramp (any ramp) proves to be almost impossible without advanced machinery, there is another problem. In order to ensure that all the corners of the pyramid would meet correctly at the top (the point), you would need to have clear sight lines. Placing a continuous ring of ramps around the exterior of the pyramid would block these sight lines. In essence, you would be working blind.[24]

Cranes have also been suggested, though not frequently at this point in the game. There simply would not be enough room on the edges of the pyramid to support the type of weight these cranes would need to hold. New theories always abound, but don't buy any of the "Mystery

---

[23] See the *National Geographic* documentary, "The Great Pyramid Mystery Solved," at about 6:00 minutes in.
[24] Ibid, 8:30.

Solved!" material out there on the web. Those are advertising ploys; we *still* don't know how they did it.

Adding complexity to the problem, we have to consider that the pyramids could not have been built in isolation. As science writer, Owen Jarus, put it: the formation of the pyramids ". . . required constructing not just the pyramids, but also the temples, boat pits and cemeteries located near the enormous structures."[25] There would be an incredible amount of materials and labor that went in to all of this. But it gets even better. While it is perhaps the most famous of our ancient marvels, the Great Pyramid is by no means the only example of superb primitive engineering coming from ancient Egypt. As Phillip Coppens has pointed out, "The Great Pyramid . . . tends to be seen in isolation. But it is not. The Pyramid of Khafre next to it is almost as big, as is the Red Pyramid at Dashur."[26] We have not one massive pyramid to explain, but three.

Never mind the fact that the pyramid complex at Giza—consisting of Khufu, Khafre, and Menkaure—also happens to align with Orion's Belt, a feat that would require impressive astronomical understanding. More mystifying—and more indicative of the fact that the same intelligences were at work all over the world—is that both the Hopi Mesas and the pyramid complex in Teotihuacán also align with Orion's Belt.[27] Bear in mind that the Hopi Mesas are found in Arizona, and that Teotihuacán is located in Mexico. This means that ancient civilizations from Egypt, North America, and South America shared this fascination (and knowledge) of something that they simply should not have been able to understand. Were they all visited by the same beings? It seems rather plausible to me. Perhaps that is even *necessarily* true.

So, the ancients were able to build amazing structures—structures we still struggle to fully comprehend thousands of years later—but perhaps we will later discover that it wasn't so difficult after all. That is

---

[25] Owen Jarus, "How Were the Egyptian Pyramids Built?"
[26] Phillip Coppens, *The Ancient Alien Question,* 89.
[27] Ibid. 280.

exceedingly doubtful. We know full well what it takes to move massive stones, because we too have done it before. As recent as 2012, a giant megalith that would later become the sculpture known as "Levitated Mass," was transported 105 miles through California. Weighing 340 tons (680,000 pounds), it was shipped from a quarry in Riverside to the Los Angeles County Museum of Art. It was a relatively easy process; all it involved was workers from about 100 utility crews, a 1.4 million pound crane, a 44-axel tractor-trailer rig possessing 2400 horsepower, and eleven nights of navigation.[28]

In comparison, Ancient Egypt's Ramesseum weighs 1,000 tons and Rome's Trilithon stones weigh 800 tons *each*, respectively. Levitated Mass—the 340-ton megalith at the Los Angeles County Museum of Art—pales in size to these ancient stones (and certain others). Again, relocating Levitated Mass required some of our best and most advanced technology. But the ancient peoples supposedly moved massive stones, cut them to exact specifications, and placed them high on top of one another in very precise ways, with nothing more than slave labor and primitive tools. How can any honest person really believe that?

To be sure, much of the architecture described thus far seems to become more complex the more we look it. But there are other reasons to believe there were hyper-intelligent beings at work within the ancient world. The repetition of certain motifs within ancient cultures provides further reason to be curious. I will spend more time discussing this point later on, but it is worth mentioning here that the issue Erich Von Däniken has referred to as "connections between continents" is very real. We saw this earlier with the various structures that align with Orion's Belt, but there is more. Cultures existing at similar times, on entirely different continents, often depicted seeing beings with "gleaming faces," "radiant auras around their heads," large eyes, eye-wear, round heads, halos, and other similar physical characteristics.[29] The problem, of course, is that

---

[28] See the article, "Ancient Engineering mysteries: How did Ancient Mankind move and cut megalithic blocks of stone?" for additional information.

many of these cultures had no realistic way of collaborating with one another. At least not on their own.

The evidence goes on and on. A growing number of scholars and researchers have documented an almost innumerable list of head-scratching—if not materialistically unexplainable—events in our history. To those who have been studying these connections and phenomena, the unusual nature of things like the "UFOs that stopped play" and the precision design of ancient structures comes as no surprise. But for the great many people who are not so familiar with events and architecture of this nature, it should come as a shock. It *should* cause us to be honest with ourselves, and ask how we might best explain the evidence. It appears that we must either acknowledge that civilizations like the ancient Egyptians were more technologically savvy than we are today—which sounds absurd in a world where most of us are walking around with a miniature computer in our pockets—or we must accept that these cultures had help.

Perhaps the best explanation is that these cultures were way *ahead* of their time because they were informed by those who existed way *before* their time. Like many have chosen to do, we could opt for purely naturalistic explanations—meaning unguided, ordinary causes—for the immense number of UFO sightings throughout history, the incredible architecture of the ancient peoples, and all of the rest, if we so desire. However, ask yourself this: can *all* of these experiences be fictitious? Can we view *all* of these events as being "ordinary," materialistically-explainable occurrences?

Again, we should remember that if even one of the countless stories of foreign flying beings or extraterrestrial visitation is valid—just one—then there are indeed extraterrestrial beings within this dimension or another. Lastly, we are left wondering why groups that were separated by tremendous distances were infatuated with depicting (deifying, really) a separate set of beings in precisely the same ways. I for one find it

---

[29] Erich Von Däniken, *Evidence of the Gods*, 69-82.

incredibly improbable that there is nothing strange going on with any of this.

The overall wealth of evidence points to something that some people truly wish to affirm and others are horrified to even entertain: we have been visited by highly sophisticated, otherworldly (or as I will suggest, *otherrealmly*) beings: not just once or twice, but many, many times. As the preceding events and structures illustrate, these visitations are not confined to the distant past, either. It is still happening all over the globe, if we are willing to see it. Only those viewing the world through the blind eyes of overt religious skepticism or dogmatic materialism could even dare to chalk it all up to chance or natural processes. Many do, of course. There is always a possible naturalistic explanation to offer for all of these discoveries and events. Things like hallucination, wishful thinking, wind and water erosion, all other manner of "natural phenomena," and a plethora of alternative explanations, are always there to ensure us that nothing unusual *really* happened.

As long as there is another "explanation" left to turn to on the rolodex—and the possibilities are endless, though most are not rational—these events will never be viewed honestly or truthfully. But as a person of deep religious faith who has spent years engaged in detailed Bible study, I can no longer sweep all of this under the rug. As a truth-seeker, I can no longer turn a blind eye to all of these occurrences and archaeological findings. The overall sum of evidence for extraterrestrial visitation is simply too overwhelming, too pronounced, and too well-documented for quiet dismissals.

While it is probably impossible to have absolute clarity about what occurred with these odd sightings and works of engineering genius, the reality that there are other beings—beings who were/are vastly superior to us in many respects—involved in the greater picture of our existence seems unavoidable. Clearly, something happened. More appropriately, *someone* happened. While I will provide more and more reasons to believe this as the book progresses, it is important to take a quick pause, in order to bring another topic into the fold. This will prove to be a vital issue within the scope of the book: perhaps, *the* vital issue. One of the primary questions posed to all of us who are willing to at least go this far is, who is this someone or someone/s? Who, or perhaps *what*, are these intelligent beings?

Defining the "Gods"

At the very moment I started to really investigate the myriad examples of extraterrestrial contact in our world, a number of theological concerns materialized for me. I recall a fishing trip I took with my father and brother. After a long day of searching for fish (and catching a few), we settled into our hotel for the night. Having flipped through the channels for a good twenty minutes, we came to a movie that immediately captured our collective attention. The movie was called *Prometheus*, and it is not for the faint of heart.

The central plot of *Prometheus* is that a future group of technologically advanced human beings goes in search of a distant planet, which is thought to hold clues about our creator/s. After arriving on the planet—and encountering a number of extraordinarily strange and lethal creatures—the group finally discovers what they had set out to find. There, lying unconscious within a cryogenic chamber of sorts, is one of the beings who had spawned the human race. There was our "creator"— one of our "gods." Having found this being, the hyper-intelligent android on the ship awakens the being and begins its best attempt at communicating with it in its own dialect. The crew's hope was very simple—perhaps this entity could answer life's deepest questions. Maybe it could explain our origins, why we are here, where it all is heading, and even why our creator/s had abandoned us. If anyone could answer these questions, it would surely be this being.

For the crew aboard the Prometheus, unfortunately, this "god" did not intend to reveal such mysteries. Instead, it began a deadly assault on the crew while on route to launching its superior spacecraft. Its intent in doing so was even more ominous: return to Earth and destroy the creatures that its race had once produced. I will not spoil the ending for those who have not seen it—at least not yet—but it was not the ending that kept me up that night; what disturbed me was the reality that the creator they had discovered cared absolutely nothing for humanity. Worse, it had decided that we ought to be destroyed once and for all.

As the movie certainly insinuates, this entity was more than capable of completing the task. Had humanity been created as nothing more than an experiment? Are we here only for the amusement of the gods, or for some completely selfish purpose? Are we utterly disposable? While *Prometheus* is a science fiction film—making it very easy to dismiss for those of us living in reality—some of the questions it raises are not actually so fictitious or outlandish. Not if we really think about it.

What is *our* Creator—the God of the Bible—actually like? What type of entity are we talking about? Is God a physical being or an immaterial being? Does God dwell somewhere out in the distant recesses of outer space, or in some completely different dimension or realm? Did God form our world out of pre-existing materials, whether that is from another universe or another realm, as the creation *ex materia* view suggests?[30] If not, are we talking about a being who can bring all material things into existence from literally nothing, as the creation *ex nihilo* view posits?[31] These are just a few of the questions that human beings have pondered and studied since we were placed on Earth by our Creator.

The most ancient cultures surely entertained these very questions. Every religion throughout history has essentially set out to answer these riddles. To be sure, many, *many* different answers have emerged. For the Christian, it may feel as though these types of questions have been settled

---

[30] Creation *ex materia* is the belief that all time, matter, space, etc., was brought forth from pre-existing materials.
[31] In complete opposition to creation *ex materia*, creation *ex nihilo* is the belief that all time, matter, space, etc. was brought forth literally from nothing.

for nearly two millennia. As one who believes whole-heartedly in Jesus Christ and the veracity of the biblical texts, I have to wonder how the "Ancient Alien Question"—as Philip Coppens has called it—meshes with the metanarrative of Scripture.[32] I think you may be rather surprised to see just how much sense these two ideas can make when viewed together. When "ancient astronaut theory" (sometimes called "ancient alien hypothesis") meets biblical teaching, both the similarities and the differences can be shocking.

However, in order to see this connection, we have to be very clear about what kind of beings we are talking about. Are the extraterrestrials that have contacted us of the same fashion as those depicted within the movie *Prometheus*: beings that are essentially just more intelligent and advanced versions of us, who arose somewhere else within the universe? Are these beings like the normative Judeo-Christian understanding of God and the angelic beings: immaterial entities that possess powers beyond human understanding? Or, are we dealing with beings that are perhaps some blend of both? As this book unfolds, I think it will become apparent that it is actually the third option that may make the best sense of things.

Throughout the rest of this book, you will often read the phrase, *we already believe this.* The reason is that many of the ideas being entertained by ancient astronaut theorists not only correlate with what we read in the Bible, but often make much better sense of biblical ideas than just about anything else. At times, of course, the opposite is the case. The overall result, as I see it, is the fortification of the Christian faith and the trustworthiness of the Bible. In turn, it also validates many of the views held within ancient astronaut theory. Should we completely buy into every theory out there? Of course not. Some of the ideas we might see on a show like *Ancient Aliens* are just utterly absurd (the recurring suggestion

---

[32] Philip Coppens has actually written an entire book bearing this title (*The Ancient Alien Question*). Among other things, the book continues the task of asking how we can explain the existence of incredibly advanced ancient civilizations apart from extraterrestrial guidance.

that the moon is actually a giant spaceship comes to mind).[33] But we should not throw the baby out with the bath water, so to speak. There is quite a lot of truth involved in some of these concepts.

In all of the examples I have mentioned thus far—and in those to come—the best explanation is that intelligent beings from somewhere beyond our world are responsible. Rather than viewing the suggestion of "aliens" or "extraterrestrials" as sacrilegious or outright kooky (as I once did), we ought to truly consider that this information could provide valuable evidence for the existence of God and the angelic beings. Certainly, most people think of aliens or extraterrestrials as creatures that dwell somewhere out in space, on some other planet. To some, these terms are errantly limited to that strict definition. But in the truest sense, isn't God an extraterrestrial of sorts? Wouldn't both God and the angels exist outside of, and beyond, our planet? When you think about it, the term "extraterrestrial" casts a very wide net.

As this book unfolds, the evidence that we are not alone in existence will continue to mount. In investigating all of the issues presented here, I have never been more certain of that fact. What has been offered thus far is truly just the tip of the iceberg. In addition to this, the entire picture of who the beings are that have contacted us throughout history should become clearer and clearer. It is important not only to see that intelligent fingerprints are detectible in almost every aspect of our world, but also to begin to establish whose fingerprints these are. As we progress through these issues, ask yourself: do these appear to be the fingerprints of interplanetary beings, or the fingerprints of those from another realm or dimension altogether? *Who are the extraterrestrials?* That is the central question in all of this.

---

[33] See *Ancient Aliens*, S11E11 for a great example of this thinking.

Chapter Two

A World of Contact

In the first chapter, the overall purpose was to provide a succinct flurry of very solid evidence for the existence of extraterrestrial—in the most general sense of the word—beings. In essence, this should have provided sensible reasons as to why you (the reader) should at least entertain this prospect. Hopefully, some of this has peaked your interest. Moreover, the pivotal question about the identities of these extraterrestrials was planted. In this chapter, I will move on to providing many more reasons to believe that we are not the only intelligent beings in existence. This will be done by illustrating some of the incredible connections that existed among things like the many ancient creation accounts and flood narratives, as well as by underlining some of the powerful scientific evidence that corroborates the belief in otherworldly entities. We begin this chapter by examining our own beginnings: with how it all got started.

Our Origins

One of the most obvious ways that extraterrestrials have reached out to the world is in creation. In this, I do not mean through the incredible complexity and "fine-tuning" that is apparent within our world, and its placement in the universe. To be sure, there is plenty of that to talk about. For the moment, I am concerned with the ways in which the higher beings have reached out to humanity and revealed the basic facts surrounding our origins. When we begin to investigate the various creation accounts posited by ancient cultures and religions, we cannot help but see striking similarities. One might even conclude that these similarities are far too widespread to be coincidental.

Take, for example, the ancient Babylonian account, as read in the *Enuma Elish*. The tablets containing this creation account date to 1100 BCE, but they are almost certainly later copies of earlier stories.[34] The opening line on the first of the "Seven Tablets" records the following:

> "When in the height heaven was not named, And the earth beneath did not yet bear a name, And the primeval Apsu, who begat them, And chaos, Tiamut, the mother of them both. Their waters were mingled together . . ."[35]

A couple of things stand out in these few lines. We have both "heaven" and "earth" mentioned, with heaven clearly being above the earth (in the "height"). We also have the presence of water at the very onset of creation. Perhaps most importantly, there is the allusion to a creation brought forth from "chaos."

The Zoroastrian creation account, dating back to around the sixth century BC, holds that there was a beginning to our realm, with the one "wise Lord" Ahura Mazda existing in Endless Light and the Evil Spirit Ahriman living in Absolute Darkness.[36] Further, the account holds that Ahura Mazda created plant life, animal life, and then mankind, *in that precise order*. Doesn't this sound strangely familiar? The Norse cosmogony also proposes a chaotic primordial state. Prior to the formation of an orderly universe, nothing existed but the "Ginnungagap," which is essentially a bottomless abyss.[37] One of the ancient Chinese creation stories concerning Pangu—the creator of all things—also describes a universe once existing only in chaos, with the "heaven" and the "earth" nebulously jumbled together.[38] Pangu is said to have slept in an "egg"—an explanation

---

[34] Joshua J. Mark's, "Enuma Elish - The Babylonian Epic of Creation."
[35] *Enuma Elish: Epic of Creation*, Tablet 1.
[36] Jacques Duchesne-Guillemin, "Zoroastrianism."
[37] Dan McCoy, "Ginnungagap."
[38] E.C. Rammel, "Pangu and the Chinese Creation Story."

strangely resembling (to some) modern conceptions of Big Bang cosmology—in which he awakens and realizes he is trapped.

Cracking the "egg," Pangu splits the shell and creates the sky above and the earth below. Thus, the heavens and the earth are separated. Even the ancient Greeks referred to a creation formed out of chaos, with light coming forth out of the darkness, and the earth following thereafter.[39] Apparently, there was widespread agreement between often geographically and temporally separated cultures on issues like the once-chaotic state of the universe, the existence of water at the earliest of times, the separation of heaven and earth at creation, and often even the creative progression from plants, to animals, to human beings.

For those coming from the ancient astronaut background, there is the tendency to view these creation stories, and the incredible similarities between *parts* of them, as being valid depictions of what once happened with our universe. The difference between their views and those held by religious believers is pretty straightforward: the ancient astronaut theorists tend to believe that the "gods" were misidentified by those who both witnessed them and received this information about our origins. In their view, a god is really an entity from another planet; ancient people had mistaken a space being (an ancient astronaut) for a divine or metaphysical being. Giorgio Tsoukalos—one of ancient astronaut theory's most prominent figures—summarized this view very clearly in an episode of *Ancient Aliens*, saying:

> ". . . in my opinion, angels do not exist. Angels were merely a misinterpretation of flesh and blood extraterrestrials, who descended from the sky with means of technology. And that is what these (quote, unquote) 'angels' used."[40]

---

[39] "The Creation," Greek Mythology.
[40] See "Aliens and Sacred Places" on *Ancient Aliens* (S3E3).

Clearly, that marks a profound difference between the two views of extraterrestrials at stake here: the ancient astronaut view and the biblical view.

However, let's not miss the forest for the trees. For those of us who hold that the Bible is the ultimate written expression of God to man, it is safe to say that *we already believe* most of this information about Creation. The Bible doesn't hold that Pangu is the creator god, or that he once existed in an egg balanced by the powers of Yin and Yang. But, like the Pangu account, we do believe there was a single creator God that separated the "light" from the "darkness" (Gen. 1:4). Our faith does not affirm that Apsu and Tiamat are the gods of creation and chaos, but it does affirm that God created the heavens and the earth, and that He separated the waters that existed at creation (Gen. 1:6, 9-10). Christian teaching definitely doesn't align with the notion that the "one wise Lord" Ahura Mazda existed eternally alongside of the Evil Spirit Ahriman. We do believe, however, that there is *one* "wise Lord," that there was darkness and light at creation, and that God created plant life, animal life, and then humanity—the crowned jewel of creation—in that precise order.[41]

We also believe that there is an ultimate evil entity, but not in the type of dualistic way suggested in Zoroastrianism; the Bible consistently depicts Yahweh as the most powerful entity in existence, with Satan clearly being a created subordinate. We do not believe—by any stretch of the imagination—that there is an immense and complicated pantheon of gods that periodically convene on Mt. Olympus. But we do affirm a chaotic, primordial existence in which light proceeds from the darkness (Gen. 1:2, 4), with our Earth being formed at a time thereafter (Gen. 1:9). There are undeniable similarities at play here, at least with regards to these particular ideas. It would be completely disingenuous to believe otherwise. But why is there so much overlap, and at specific points, within the

---

[41] Genesis 1:11 affirms the creation of plant life, 1:20-26 tells of the creation of the animals, and 1:27-28 discusses the creation of human beings and their appointed dominion over the earth.

traditions of these ancient cultures and their respective religions? In order to answer this question, we must press on and consider more of these connections.

Water Worlds

While the similarities within key features of the ancient creation accounts are certainly thought-provoking, the connections concerning our watery past are even more bizarre. The Bible tells of an immense flood in which God wiped humanity off the map. Becoming exceedingly angry at their consistent and egregious rebellion, God decides to destroy the world of men. Genesis 6:11-13 records the following:

> "Now the earth was corrupt in God's sight and was full of violence. God saw how corrupt the earth had become, for all the people on earth had corrupted their ways. So God said to Noah, 'I am going to put an end to all people, for the earth is filled with violence because of them. I am surely going to destroy both them and the earth'."

As the text describes, only a man named Noah and his family were allowed to survive the impending destruction. Certain pseudepigraphal (falsely attributed) works make reference to the idea that Noah was actually some type of superhuman entity, which may have had much to do with God's selection of Noah and his family in the first place.[42] Naturally, ancient astronaut theorists (among others) have gotten a

---

[42] The so-called "Book of Noah," which is referenced in the Book of Enoch, tells about Lamech's fear that he and his wife had given birth to a very different type of being. Among other things, the text records the following: "I have begotten a strange son, diverse from and unlike man, and resembling the sons of the God of heaven; and his nature is different and he is not like us, and his eyes are as the rays of the sun, and his countenance is glorious. And it seems to me that he is not sprung from me but from the angels, and I fear that in his days a wonder may be wrought on the earth." The *Book of Enoch*, chapter CVI, vv. 5-6.

lot of mileage out of this notion. The Bible, on the other hand, is adamant that Noah was indeed a man and that he was saved because of his righteous nature (Gen. 6:9).

While the Bible's portrayal of the Great Flood is undoubtedly the most popular, it is not by any stretch the only flood tradition. In fact, nearly every ancient culture had its own flood story. Besides the biblical account, the most notable version probably comes to us from the Mesopotamian *Epic of Gilgamesh*. Many believe that the *Epic of Gilgamesh* actually predates the writings of the Old Testament, and it could very well predate all other major works of ancient literature. In its introduction of Gilgamesh, the King of Uruk—who is, incidentally, part god and part man—the *Epic* makes several allusions to a great flood of destruction:

> "He saw the Secret, discovered the Hidden, he brought information of (the time) before the Flood . . . Mighty net, protector of his people, raging flood-wave who destroys even walls of stone! . . . It was he who reached by his own sheer strength Utanapishtim, the Faraway, who restored the sanctuaries that the Flood had destroyed!"[43]

Though references to the flood show up very early on, it is not really until the end of the *Epic* (Tablet IX) that we are given greater clarity concerning the event. Utanapishtim—the man commissioned by another god, named Enki, to build a massive boat that would preserve him and his family during the flood (sound familiar?)—reveals the "secret of the gods" to Gilgamesh:

> "Shuruppak, a city that you surely know, situated on the banks of the Euphrates, that city was very old, and there were gods inside it. The hearts of the Great Gods moved them to inflict the Flood . . . The gods were frightened by the Flood,

---

[43] *The Epic of Gilgamesh*, Tablet I.

and retreated, ascending to the heaven of Anu. The gods were cowering like dogs, crouching by the outer wall. Ishtar shrieked like a woman in childbirth . . . Six days and seven nights came the wind and flood, the storm flattening the land. When the seventh day arrived, the storm was pounding, the flood was a war--struggling with itself like a woman writhing (in labor). The sea calmed, fell still, the whirlwind (and) flood stopped up. I looked around all day long—quiet had set in and all the human beings had turned to clay! The terrain was as flat as a roof."[44]

While the *Epic*'s insistence that there are a great number of gods and god-like entities (Gilgamesh being one of them) involved in this particular flood story, the Bible clearly depicts the Flood as the product of one God, Yahweh, who had reached His limit with human disobedience.

Still, the similarities are striking. There is a massive flood due to divine dissatisfaction with humanity, a righteous man who builds a giant ship to escape the flood, and the preservation of human beings and civilization through this great "Ark." As previously mentioned, the *Epic of Gilgamesh* is by no means the only ancient flood story possessing similarities with the Bible's Noah and the Ark account. There are a number of ancient flood myths recorded by the ancient Chinese people, the Gun-Yu myth being the most prominent.[45] Though the accounts vary slightly, the ancient Greeks also believed in a great flood that was sent by Zeus (the "father of the gods") to destroy humanity.[46]

Clearly, flood traditions are very widespread among ancient cultures. The ancient Sumerians, who actually preceded the Babylonians,[47] also wrote about a flood: "All the windstorms, exceedingly powerful, attacked as one,

---

[44] Ibid. Tablet IX.
[45] April Holloway, "Gun-Yu and the Chinese Flood Myth."
[46] Myths Encyclopedia, "Floods."
[47] See "Sumerian Myth."

at the same time, the flood sweeps over the cult centers."[48] This meager reference to a flood indicates something very important—even the earliest cultures on record believed that there had been a giant deluge.

For those who will not accept the words of all of these prominent cultures, it is important to note that scientific endeavors have also found compelling evidence for an ancient flood (or perhaps, *floods*). In 1993, Columbia University scientists William Ryan and Walter Pitman made a scientific expedition to the Black Sea with the Russian Academy of Sciences. Utilizing sonar-imaging techniques, they were able to detect that shorelines had once been about 140 meters (nearly 460 feet) lower than they were at the time of testing.[49] The presence of a single, uniform layer of mud was also found, suggesting that a flood may well have occurred on the Black Sea. Moreover, the expedition recovered sun-bleached freshwater mollusks via sediment samples.

Using carbon-14 dating methods, they were able to tell that the mollusks from both the deepest and the shallowest layers of that sediment were only about forty years apart; the waters had not risen gradually, but rapidly. A column on Columbia News summarized their subsequent theory in the following way:

> "Ryan and Pitman believe that the sealed Bosporus strait, which acted as a dam between the Mediterranean and Black seas, collapsed when climatic warming at the close of the last glacial period and caused icecaps to melt, raising global sea level. With more than 200 times the force of Niagara Falls, the flood caused water levels in the Black Sea, which was no more than a large lake, to rise six inches per day and swallowed 60,000 square miles in less than a year."[50]

---

[48] Samuel Kramer, *History Begins at Sumer,* 153.
[49] Hannah Fairfield, "Noah's Flood."
[50] Hannah Fairfield, "Finding Noah's Flood."

In effect, it was perhaps the Mediterranean Sea that had flooded, causing the Black Sea to fill so drastically. Wouldn't that actually be the most probable biblical location of the Great Flood? After all, the Mediterranean Sea is located just west of Israel and near where the ancient biblical figures would have lived.

A number of other researchers have come to believe that there was indeed a flood of large proportions that occurred at the Black Sea, several thousand years after the last ice age. Perhaps most notably, renowned Titanic researcher, Robert Ballard, has taken a special interest in the possibility of a Black Sea flood. Ballard's overarching theory was that around 7000 BC, post ice age warming caused oceans and seas to rise, resulting in the "swelling" of the Mediterranean Sea and a subsequent push of its waters north through modern-day Turkey.[51] In fact, he too speculated that this water ended up hitting the Black Sea with a force 200 times harder than those created by the incredible Niagara Falls.[52] A 2004 expedition by a number of prominent scientists also led to the conclusion that the Black Sea was once ". . . an immense lake of black water that at one point in history began to widen in an unusually rapid way."[53]

While neither the works of Ryan and Pitman nor Robert Ballard suggested that the entire world was covered in water, they certainly suggested that a sizeable flood occurred in an area that could fall right in line with the biblical account. It is worth mentioning that the size of the Flood is seriously debated, even among those of the Christian faith. It is at least conceivable that the Flood was a local or regional flood, and that it occurred in this specific area—though there is certainly evidence that points to a global flood (discussed momentarily). While the proposition that an event of this magnitude actually occurred in the areas of the Black and Mediterranean seas is not unanimously accepted as fact—William Ryan himself has ask

---

[51] See "Ballard and the Black Sea."
[52] Ibid.
[53] Leonardo Vintini, "Noah's Ark and the Great Flood, Did it Really Happen?"

some perplexing questions about the theory—it is compelling nonetheless.[54]

While parts of these theories have somewhat fizzled out—having found no telltale signs of extremely ancient housing, only wreckage dating between about 350-550 AD—the general idea that there was indeed a type of major flooding event that occurred in the Black Sea region is still difficult to ignore.[55] Was this the site of the Great Flood? We don't know, but it certainly seems as though something of the sort happened.

While a flood at the Black Sea does not directly correlate to a global flood, there are other things that may point to such an event. The presence of marine fossils around the globe—from the highest mountain tops, to the lowest canyons, and everything in between—has been extremely well-established. In fact, not even the hardened religious skeptics in the fields of paleontology and archaeology doubt this fact (though they see no religious implications). In 2010, a mass grave site of marine life was found at Cerro Ballena (meaning "Whale Hill," in Spanish) in Chile's Atacama Desert. Yes, I said *desert*.

Among the findings were about forty whales, along with dolphins, seals, large fish, and even extinct species such as aquatic sloths and ancient dolphins.[56] North of this site, in Peru, the remains of an ancient sperm whale were found in the Pisco-Ica Desert. Other marine fossils found at the site include baleen whales, beaked whales, dolphins, sharks, turtles, seals, and seabirds.[57] A similar site in Egypt, called Wadi El Hitan ("Whale Valley," in Arabic), was designated as a UNESCO World Heritage Site in 2005, because of its treasure trove of ancient marine fossils.

Of course, deserts are not the only unexpected places where marine fossils have been unearthed; they have been found on mountain

---

[54] See Ryan's article, "Status of the Black Sea Hypothesis," for a follow-up of the 1993 findings.
[55] Robert Ballard, "Ballard and the Black Sea."
[56] See the CBC article, "Desert whale graveyard mystery solved."
[57] See Malcolm W. Browne's article, "Whale Fossils High in Andes Show How Mountains Rose from Sea."

ranges across the world. In fact, they exist all over the Himalayas, which is the world's tallest mountain range. We have even found marine fossils on the summit of Mt. Everest, which is the highest mountain point above sea level in the world. This means that fossils of marine animals exist everywhere in the world, and at every height or depth imaginable. On the face of it, the obvious conclusion should be that waters covered the globe at some point in our history. More specifically, at some point *after* marine life was abundant throughout the world.

As usual, the unapparent reason is the one most of us have been taught in our science textbooks. The ready-made scientific answer to these phenomena is that there are, of course, perfectly good materialistic explanations for all of it. When discussing the oddity of finding marine fossils high atop the Andes mountain range, the investigative team at the site—led by paleontologist Dr. Michael J. Novacek—offered the following explanation:

> "When these animals died from 15 million to 20 million years ago, their carcasses settled to the ocean floor and were embedded in submarine sediments. But since then, the violent upthrusting of the Andean chain has carried the sediments to the tops of mountains. In geological terms, the time the fossils took to rise from ocean floor to mountain top was relatively brief."[58]

In essence, this general story is the same for all of the mountain tops; they were once under the sea, and were propelled far up above the surface by the movement of the Earth's crust, through the shifting of tectonic plates. I am trying to recall the last time a gigantic mountain burst forth from the sea.

I cannot recall any such event because all of this is believed to have happened an extraordinarily long time ago, which is standard for most things that we cannot really explain in science. When in doubt, push the timeline back

---

[58] See Malcolm W. Browne's article, "Whale Fossils High in Andes Show How Mountains Rose from Sea."

as far as possible in order to muddy the waters. Millions upon millions of years ago, just about anything *could* have happened. Couched within this narrative is the belief that all of the land involved in the mountain ranges existed under the sea at the same time the ancient marine animals lived. This not only means that our mountain range formations would have to be extremely old, but that highly evolved sea creatures—like ancient whales and dolphins—had come to exist by that time. This would require that hundreds of millions of years (probably more) of evolution must have preceded the formation of nearly all of the mountain ranges on the planet. Being that our oldest mountain ranges are typically believed to be *well over* 1 billion years old, this would make the sea life deposited on them even older. See how fast that timeline can move backwards? See how quickly the stories can mount?

This problem becomes more pronounced when we factor in the reality that we have also discovered fossil remains of trees, called "polystrate fossils," that exist in various places in the world. These fossils often form "fossil forests," and are found standing upright through several strata (sediment layers). This should also cause us to take pause. Let me get this straight: trees, and even clusters of trees, stood upright for millions of years while sediment layer after sediment layer gradually covered over them? Pardon me if I am not convinced. This needed to happen very quickly, not over the course of millions (or even just thousands) of years. That is not how fossilization occurs.

Further, many of the marine animal remains we have found in deserts and on mountain tops were clearly deposited swiftly; almost suddenly, really. In many cases, the fossils are completely intact and whole, a phenomenon that only occurs if the animal is rapidly buried in sediment. This is what we would expect from something like the rushing—and then quickly receding—waters of a flood, not through much longer periods of geological shifting. Further, we know that fossilization most commonly occurs in fluvial (river/stream) or former floodplain settings.[59] Most

---

[59] I refer you to Gregory Erickson's explanation, found in the article, "What are the odds of a dead dinosaur becoming fossilized?"

animals that are not rapidly covered in sediment are never fossilized, because scavengers scatter the remains before that can take place.[60] On the whole, the existence of one or more catastrophic deluges in history seems to be more than sufficiently evident, even from a purely scientific perspective.

Clearly, the idea that water once covered the Earth (in one way or another) is well known and has been heavily researched. We know this is both a modern and an ancient issue. As noted earlier, notions of a giant flood are as old as any idea in human history. What was the cause of this catastrophic event? The ancients were adamant about the cause: divine, heavenly beings were responsible for it. While these beings go by different names—Gun-Yu, Zeus, *Yahweh*, etc.—none of these cultures believed that the flood occurred purely by natural causes. According to the ancient traditions, it was intentional. Even if we hold that the flood was simply a product of natural causes—meaning that the ancient authors misidentified the cause as "God" or the "gods"—we would be left with the questions *behind the question.* How is it that Noah, for example, could have known that he needed to construct a giant boat in order to survive the event? Who was responsible for warning those inhabitants about their impending doom?

Given these issues, it has been suggested that some type of alien or extraterrestrial being was involved in this event. In a sense, that view is quite right. As we saw in the biblical account of Noah and the Ark at the beginning of this section, *we already believe this.* We believe that God is an "extraterrestrial" being—one who is other than and transcendent from our world—do we not? We can be nearly certain of several points in all of this. The first is that there was almost certainly a Great Flood (or floods) because every prominent ancient culture affirms it, and modern science has slowly been verifying that something of the sort occurred. To call all of these accounts "myths" is truly unfair. It is quite true that many of the

---

[60] Ibid.

particulars of the flood stories differ from culture to culture, but the historical reality that there was a catastrophic deluge in the ancient Near East (and elsewhere, probably), at some point in our history, ought to be considered as being probable at this juncture.

The second point is related to the first in that there is essentially a cross-cultural consensus concerning the event. While several of the most prominent accounts were mentioned, there are actually more than three hundred ancient flood stories from around the world.[61] The third point is that there is also agreement—as far as the ancient cultures are concerned—that the Flood was caused by greater, extraterrestrial beings who were releasing the waters upon the Earth for the express purpose of destroying earthlings. Lastly, these cultures seem largely to affirm that the god/s decided to spare a remnant of human beings so that the human race could ultimately outlast the Flood.

For the purposes of this book, the most interesting part of all has to do with how all of these cultures recorded flood stories to begin with. I mean, there were not exactly many survivors of the "Great Deluge," as the ancient writings certainly point out. If we are consistent about the way we interpret these narratives, then we must acknowledge that only a small remnant of people walked off of the giant yacht—or weathered the storm anywhere—when it was all said and done.

However we wish to view the possible time period for the Flood,[62] it is highly unlikely that those who survived it went on to chronicle what had happened in any type of detail; it most certainly would have occurred prior to the time when written language was being heavily propagated (if at all). Even if they had made a written record at that time, we have most definitely lost those original sources over the last five thousand years or so. We would have lost any of the copies made as well, probably. So, how

---

[61] Christopher Snyder, "Did the Story of Noah Really Happen?"
[62] Estimates for the Flood (or smaller, ancient floods) tend to range anywhere from an extremely literalist view of Genesis—with the Flood occurring in the 2300's BC—to as early as around 9000 BC.

did later generations—probably *much* later—know so much about what had transpired? How would they know details about the ship that saved humanity? More perplexing: how would they possibly know the motives and purposes behind the event?

Are we to believe that all of the information that endured from the Flood was passed down by just a few people, to their offspring, and *that alone* lead to a detailed account of what is undoubtedly one of the greatest stories in all of human history? Exceedingly doubtful. I mean, the biblical narrative records precise instructions for how the Ark was to be constructed (Gen. 6:14-22). More than that, we are talking about people, here. At what point would the story that great, great, great, great grandpa Noah used to tell about a huge flood and a massive boat begin to strain credibility? We wouldn't be talking about a few hundred years from the date of the event to the writing down of the event, as is the case with most of the Old Testament tradition, post early Genesis. This process would have occurred within only a few decades in the case of the New Testament writings. In the case of the Flood, we would be talking about an oral tradition that must have endured for thousands of years. No, there must have been good reason to believe the story.

Maybe, and I do say *maybe*, such a thing would be possible if you were dealing with a great number of people who migrated from the flood zone to higher ground.[63] For what it's worth, accounts such as the ones we see in the *Epic of Gilgamesh* and the Bible make no mention of more than a few survivors. The authors of these texts—and perhaps those who revealed the events to them—certainly didn't feel as though everyone who was left on the ground to endure the Flood was simply able to depart to other regions. The notion of a Flood that wiped out almost all of humanity and all terrestrial creatures—even if only regionally—would probably never pass muster for the next several *thousand* years unless (1)

---

[63] Scientists William Ryan and Walter Pitman suggested that such a thing may have explained how the various legends of the Great Flood were perpetuated for several thousand years prior to a written record. See Hannah Fairfield's article, "Noah's Flood."

there was a great deal of truth to it, and (2) some objective onlookers revealed the events to future generations of human beings. The same should be said about all of the events involved in the creation accounts.

Further, what about the widespread notion that a massive ship was involved in all of this? A ship even close to the size of the one described in Genesis 6:15-16 certainly wasn't going to be built *after* everyone saw the waters rising! It is just as Jesus once remarked concerning the nature of his coming and the end of the age:

> "As it was in the days of Noah, so it will be at the coming of the Son of Man. For in the days before the flood, people were eating and drinking, marrying and giving in marriage, up to the day Noah entered the ark; and they knew nothing about what would happen until the flood came and took them all away."[64]

Jesus was right—an event of this magnitude would have caught nearby civilizations by surprise, simply washing them away. But it is said that Noah knew in advance. The obvious question we ought to be asking is, who warned Noah about the coming Flood? Anyone who was going to make a giant ship in order to escape the coming deluge must have been notified well in advance. Period. But who could have had such understanding?

Being that the people of that day and age certainly didn't possess advanced weather tracking equipment—things like satellites, specially equipped planes, unmanned aircrafts, drones, and the like[65]—the chances that they had detected the gargantuan storm system on their own, and in a sufficient time frame allowing them to build the vessel, are slim to none. That's probably being too generous. It must have been an objective onlooker possessing tremendous knowledge; one who was able to know that the Flood was coming without fear of being destroyed by it. Further,

---

[64] Matthew 24:37-38.
[65] See Oskin's article, "Incredible Technology: How to Track Hurricanes."

this being must have known what type of vessel needed to be built in order to withstand that event. And of course, *we already believe this.* The Bible affirms that God directly told Noah about the impending catastrophe, and also how to craft the Ark that would save them (Gen. 6:13-17).

Moreover, the very fact that the "flood myths" ever got off the ground to begin with—much less that they have persisted so prevalently ever since—is at least plausible evidence that extraterrestrials were involved. Some being (or group of beings) must have shared the basic logistics of the Flood, as well as details like the Ark's exact dimensions, to those who came after its initial survivors. These beings were perhaps involved in the event, and they were most certainly involved in making sure that we never forgot both *that* it happened and *why* it happened.

We already believe this as well, being that every orthodox Christian tradition holds that the Spirit of God inspired—revealed what only a transcendent being could reveal—various authors to write about events that had transpired well into the past: sometimes the very distant past (no human beings were present at the earliest events of Creation, certainly). But if you can imagine, discussion of the flood stories actually requires us to ask even more perplexing questions. Chiefly, we are left to wonder about what happened to humanity after this cataclysmic event.

Globetrotters?

If we subscribe to a very literal view of the deluge accounts—as the prominent ancient cultures described it—we are left with a small number of people that must have propagated the human race and populated the world. If one chooses to ignore the high probability that something like the Great Flood (or floods) we read about within the Bible and a plethora of other ancient texts really happened, there would still be a rather difficult problem to contend with. Flood or no Flood, how did the earliest civilizations arise on different spots of the globe to begin with?

Without an intrinsic geographical knowledge of planet Earth, and no way of flying great distances,[66] shouldn't they have largely remained centrally located? At least for a very long time, certainly. If they had developed ships that were capable of carrying people thousands of miles across the open sea, could that really explain how human civilization spread around the world? These questions are potentially problematic. Chiefly, they are problematic for two reasons: they assume that everyone started off in the same place, and that they slowly dispersed from there. The "Cradle of Life," as it is often called, is *assumed* to have been the sole birthplace of the human race. From there, of course, humans supposedly spread across the globe at half the speed of smell. But is that really true?

In *any* evolutionary theory that affirms Darwin's notion of universal common ancestry—whereby all living organisms are related by a single family tree—human beings should have arisen from a more primitive ape-like ancestor at a particular spot in the world. Under no circumstances could this exact event have occurred multiple times in various spots. This is at least true in traditional, evolutionary understandings that accept universal common ancestry. I have something else to say about this momentarily. But even if we grant a full-blown evolutionary account of life, it would immediately result in a great many problems within the present discussion alone. Specifically, how could human beings have set up civilizations across the world, when that would have required them to traverse distances they could not have covered at that point in time?

Both mainstream science and most of the world's religions agree that there was a first human being who existed alongside of a second, and that we can all trace our lineage back to these people. In Judeo-Christian thought, we know the world's first couple as Adam and Eve. In the

---

[66] I say *great distances* because of what some have actually proposed about the ancient peoples who built the Nazca Lines. Jim Woodman and Julian Nott constructed a primitive hot-air balloon in an effort to show that the ancient peoples responsible for the Nazca Lines could possibly have produced them by such a means. Even if balloons would have worked, and they could have created them, there is no question that relocating entire groups of people through the continents would have been out of the question in such a craft. See Nott's website, https://nott.com/nazca/ for more information.

scientific world, this religious terminology has been copied in the terms "Y-chromosomal Adam" and "Mitochondrial Eve." It's scarcely possible to find a belief system that does not affirm the existence of a first man and a first woman. But this ought to be expected. How could there not have been a first man and a first woman, at some point in time? It's an undeniable, logical necessity.

But the thing that bothers me is what happened afterwards. Subsequent to the arrival of the first human beings on planet Earth, something incredible happened. You see, we don't have a historical record of just one group of people who lived in some isolated location for thousands of years, slowly dispersing from there. Rather, we have a historical record of scattered groups of people who existed around the globe at a very early time: perhaps at the earliest of times. In fact, many archaeological anthropologists now believe that the most ancient civilizations in human history arose independent of (and perhaps even parallel to) one another.[67] In other words, human civilizations seemed to appear around the world very quickly, and not over the course of many thousands of years. Of course, this realization is leagues apart from what most of us have heard throughout our lifetimes.

We all know that the ancient aboriginal peoples (the earliest Australians) were the very first civilization of Homo sapiens, some 50,000 years ago.[68] Well, that's what some authorities tell us, anyway. In reality, it was probably the ancient Chinese that first existed as a certified civilization, perhaps as early as 80,000 years ago.[69] But that's not the consensus opinion, of course. Everyone who studies anthropology and archaeology can tell you that human civilization first arose somewhere in Africa . . . or was it the Middle East? Yes, the ancient Mesopotamians

---

[67] See the article "Cradle of Civilization," in Wikipedia for a good introduction into this idea.
[68] Christopher Klein, "DNA Study Finds Aboriginal Australians World's Oldest Civilization."
[69] Jeffrey Kluger, "Here's Proof That the First Modern Humans Were Chinese."

came first, right? No, no, no: human civilization arose "out of Asia." In truth, you can find quality thinkers who have made the case for all of these possibilities.

Like the issues surrounding abiogenesis (how life first arose) and the plethora of evolutionary theories out there today, the rise of human civilization is still shrouded in mystery; it's all about as clear as smoke. For so many years, we were told that modern human beings descended from some ape-like ancestor in the jungles of Africa, and that they ever-so-slowly disseminated across the planet. But if it all started with a pair of human beings who came to exist at a particular place in the world, how is there a historical record of human beings who existed all around the globe at about the same time?

As I said earlier: without an intrinsic geographical knowledge of the planet and no way of travelling great distances with any real efficiency, shouldn't they have remained at least somewhat centrally located? I mean, it took European settlers nearly one thousand years to send someone to the "new world." Of course, what Christopher Columbus found in 1492 was that people already existed there: and they had for a *very* long time.[70] Did the most ancient Native Americans (the Paleo-Indians) develop a Santa Maria long before the Europeans did—whereby they shuttled their entire population to North America—or were they there by some other means?

Even if the earliest people had developed a great many ships that were seaworthy enough to traverse vast oceans—and developed them exceedingly early in their histories—did they really relocate their entire cultures in such a way? I can imagine how that dialogue must have played out. "Hey, you take your group thousands of miles that way. And you: go take your people thousands of miles that way. We'll stay here. Good luck!"

---

[70] See Stefan's article, "Who Were the First Americans?" for more information on this matter.

This is not to undermine the impressive ship building of some of the ancient cultures. We know the Egyptians, Chinese, Romans, Vikings, and others, crafted very capable boats in their respective time periods. But there seems to be a major gap somewhere in this story. In order to spread across the globe, all of those people must have had advanced ship building techniques at a *very* early time. Of course, we know that these cultures each developed these techniques independent of one another, as their civilizations advanced. It's somewhat of a chicken or the egg question, is it not?

The Vikings weren't building their longships at the inception of their civilization. The ancient Chinese weren't sailing around in their Junk ships from the beginning. None of the ancient cultures just started out with ships that could navigate the open oceans. These things took time! Yet, many of them were able to ultimately achieve this, and *all* of them appear to have existed on separate continents beforehand. How? Whenever they did finally venture to other lands, as the Vikings did when they traveled "west" to England, they found many groups who had existed there for a long time (as Columbus did in the Americas).

Then again, maybe the ancient peoples didn't need ships at all. Perhaps they simply walked across giant land bridges that supposedly existed all over the world, some tens of thousands of years ago. This is another fine materialistic explanation on the old rolodex and, like most of them, it is not overly convincing. The issue of how humans came to inhabit the globe, like most other origin discussions, involves a lot of speculation and not a great deal of agreement. The most popular view of how the first people arrived in the Americas has been that they crossed on an ancient land bridge, towards the end of the last ice age. This strip, called the Bering Land Bridge, is thought to have allowed people from Eurasia to travel into North America, as the lowering in water depths exposed a large land bridge between continents.[71]

---

[71] Megan Gannon, "Study: the First Americans Didn't Arrive by the Bering Land Bridge."

It was on this land bridge that the ancient Paleo-Indian culture, commonly referred to as the "Clovis" peoples, were thought to have lived and traveled. Naturally, many people have challenged this view over the years. In 2016, researcher Mikkel Pedersen and a group of associates published a paper in *Nature*, suggesting that the Bering Land Bridge was probably not the way the first settlers traveled into North America.[72] Using sediment samples drilled from Charlie Lake and Spring Lake (both in western Canada), they were able to reconstruct what environmental conditions may have been like in the area near the end of the last ice age.

They found that the likely time period that the land bridge would have been conducive to human travel was around 12,600 years ago. This is problematic to the Bering Land Bridge theory because, as they noted in the study, "We know conclusively that human groups were in the interior before that date."[73] Their overall conclusion was that the Bering Land Bridge may well have been used by someone, but not by the earliest settlers. They were already there, somehow.

In an article discussing the group's findings, science writer Megan Gannon added the following information on the topic:

> "Alternate migration routes have been put forth in the past, such as the controversial Solutrean hypothesis, which posits that the first Americans actually came from Europe, not Asia, via a North Atlantic route. But many anthropologists now favor a Pacific coastal route to explain how the first people got to the Americas, though more research is needed to fully understand how these intrepid settlers traveled (perhaps by boat)."[74]

---

[72] See Pedersen's (et al.) article, "Postglacial viability and colonization in North America's ice-free corridor."
[73] Ibid.
[74] Megan Gannon, "Study: the First Americans Didn't Arrive by the Bering Land Bridge."

Quite right: we need more research. But we seem to be getting closer to the, "well, the ancient people got here by crossing *some* ancient land bridge" theory as the days go by. Maybe it was this land bridge, at this time. Maybe it was that land bridge, at time. Perhaps they arrived via boats after all, which gets back to my chicken or the egg issue from earlier. This sounds eerily similar to the way the "evolution blob"—a term we could use to explain the many competing theories that are smashed into one—is now viewed in the scientific community.[75] *Something* happened, and it didn't involve a deity; we know that!

The story appears to be the same across the globe. Similar land bridges are believed to have existed near Africa, the North Atlantic, South America, Central America, the Indian Ocean, and even Australia. But as usual, this view has many other assumed beliefs couched within it. We must first believe that Pangaea—the name given to describe the concept that the continents once formed a continuous land mass—is an accurate scientific hypothesis, and that our Earth is more than four billion years old. Clearly, we know there is debate that exists about these two notions, and isotopic dating techniques have proven to be very unreliable when dealing with issues so far back into the past. Recurring here is also the assumption of some type of complete evolutionary story, in which every organism on the planet shares a common ancestry, including Homo sapiens. As we progressed and reproduced, groups of us either separated from the others or were separated by natural barriers.

The land bridge view seems to be a necessary story, if we are to believe this type of evolutionary narrative. The result is another place where additional stories must be compounded, in order to make sense of the ones we already have. Concerning the land bridge theories, it is just as researcher William R. Corliss once wrote:

---

[75] This reality is very clearly articulated throughout Wayne Rossiter's book, *Shadow of Oz: Theistic Evolution and the Absent God*. See all of chapter 4, and page 149 especially.

> ". . . whenever geologists and paleontologists were at a loss to explain the obvious transoceanic similarities of life that they deduced from the fossil records, they sharpened their pencils and sketched land bridges between appropriate continents."[76]

We frequently do the same type of thing, when filling in "the gaps" in particular fossil records. It is funny how a few pieces of bone can turn into just about anything you want them to.

I mentioned earlier that evolutionary theories, historically, have not entertained the idea that Homo sapiens (or our direct ancestors) originated numerous times in history. The reasons why are pretty straightforward. The first is that multiple origins for ancient hominids would be absurdly improbable on an evolutionary view of history. The circumstances that would have brought our type of species into existence would be nearly impossible (completely impossible, I think) to duplicate. There are just too many factors at play, not least of which are the numerous random mutations that would have to occur in order to produce something like us. Second, going the route of multiple origins for the human race would pose an enormous problem to the notion of universal common ancestry. If we cannot trace our ancestry back through one line of primates, but must look to multiple lines, then one of the foundational pieces of the evolutionary story can be thrown out the window. At this point, I personally have no doubt that it should be.

If it is any indication of just where researchers are with trying to explain how and where human beings came to exist, consider a recent study performed by a group of esteemed archaeologists. Oxford University archaeologist, Dr. Eleanor Scerri, along with her group of international researchers, believes the long-standing view that Homo sapiens came about at one place on the globe (typically in east Africa) is incorrect. As Scerri remarked, "This single origin, single population view has stuck in people's mind[s] ... but the way we've been thinking about it is too simplistic."[77] While there are many

---

[76] See William R. Corliss', *Mysteries Beneath the Sea*, chapter five, for more information on this.

technical aspects to their research, the overall thrust of their findings is that the telltale characteristics of human beings—like a globular brain case, a chin, delicate brows, and smaller faces—seem to have appeared in different places and at different times.[78]

In essence, there were multiple populations of ancient humans that developed traits in isolation for many millennia, and then united with one another after changes in climate allowed them to do so. What resulted, ultimately, was modern human beings (us). But if there were so many different populations of ancient hominids, why do we see only one today? If evolution can so easily produce these, why isn't that still happening? Worse yet, this objection would apply to all species of animals that have ever existed.

Clearly, this view stands in complete contrast to most historical explanations, which regard Homo sapiens as arising through one line of ancient hominids, at one place in the world, and at one time in history. But this is what an honest look at the evidence yielded for the group of researchers. Scientifically speaking, we don't know where, when, why, or how human beings originated. The same thing applies to how we came to be located across the seven continents.

This may sound like an overly harsh criticism of some of our most treasured scientific theories, but that is not the intent. I simply wish to show that we have not really answered our most foundational questions: how life began (discussed later), how it diversified, how human beings came to live across the globe, and others. It is disappointing that we are told that all of this has been explained. It is equally disappointing that we so often accept the *faith* claim that "we will eventually have scientific explanations for everything, even if we do not currently." Not only is that "science of the gaps"—as opposed to the "god of the gaps" argument so often used against theists—but that claim is no different than those made by religious followers from many backgrounds. Saying "someday," and putting scientific placeholders into our gaps, does not explain what we see

---

[77] See Devlin's article, "No single birthplace of mankind, say scientists."
[78] Ibid.

today. More than that, most of these scientific hypotheses are absolutely sure to change. What is "true" today will not be tomorrow. What we are asked to believe now will likely be obsolete in the future. That is a fact as sure as life itself.

Speaking of scrutinized religious ideas, there do happen to be a few that pertain to this topic. The question is still on the table here: how did human beings come to exist across the globe, and at what truly appears to be a very early time in our history? How is it that the ancient Chinese, the Aborigines, the early Mesopotamians, the Paleo-Indian people, and civilizations from other parts of the world, came to exist in such diverse locations as far back as we can tell? If the theories (of which there are many) about an extremely gradual movement of peoples from a single ancestral location (which we are not sure of), by some means (which we are also not sure of), do not seem to adequately explain the situation, what are we left with? Simply put, we are left not with an extremely gradual process of separation, but with a rapid scattering of peoples across the face of the Earth.

That idea is, of course, anathema (accursed) within the scientific community. It flies in the face of almost every hypothesis out there. And yet, it would actually be quite consistent with what we know about the origins of human civilization. This view would best explain the evidence. It would also be the explanation given by those who were closest to the source: the ancient peoples themselves. The Mayans believed they were placed in their location by their gods, who came from the Pleiades constellation. This is assuredly one of the reasons why their temple complex at Tikal corresponds with that particular constellation. The Aboriginals believed that they were the descendants of the spirit beings, who came from the sky and created all living creatures. The various groups of Aboriginals also believed that their 250 (or more) various languages were the direct product of their creators.[79]

---

[79] For more information on this, please see Kiger's article, "Australian Aboriginal Creation Stories."

These stories certainly had variations among the different ancient cultures, but on the whole, the view that human beings and their languages were the product of divine beings is well-established. The Hebrew people—the ancient Jews—had their own view of things, but it largely corresponded with the others. At least, it is consistent with the idea that the various tribes of people were physically placed where they were by transcendent powers. Naturally, this is also the Christian and Muslim view of how this occurred.

The Bible records this event in its account of the "Tower of Babel." After the Great Flood—which all other major cultures attest to, in one way or another—humanity had repopulated the region we were spawned in. But things did not go overly well, even after that horrifying wake-up call. Genesis 11:1-9 records the following:

> "Now the whole earth used the same language and the same words. It came about as they journeyed east, that they found a plain in the land of Shinar and settled there. They said to one another, 'Come, let us make bricks and burn them thoroughly.' And they used brick for stone, and they used tar for mortar. They said, 'Come, let us build for ourselves a city, and a tower whose top will reach into heaven, and let us make for ourselves a name, otherwise we will be scattered abroad over the face of the whole earth.' The Lord came down to see the city and the tower which the sons of men had built. The Lord said, 'Behold, they are one people, and they all have the same language. And this is what they began to do, and now nothing which they purpose to do will be impossible for them. Come, let Us go down there and confuse their language, so that they will not understand one another's speech.' So the Lord scattered them abroad from there over the face of the whole earth; and they stopped building the city. Therefore its name was called Babel,

because there the Lord confused the language of the whole earth; and from there the Lord scattered them abroad over the face of the whole earth."

There is something very important to notice here: this record goes out of its way to mention that people were scattered around the whole Earth. As a matter of fact, it states this four times in only nine verses. Biblically speaking—and this would be true on any serious evolutionary view—all people were at one point living together at a particular spot on the globe. Then, what do you know, there were people all over the place. The Bible tells us that this was no accident. Nor was it some very gradual process, whereby people slowly disseminated around the continents. The heavenly beings were responsible for this; it was God's direct action.

Coming from someone who has both studied and taught the Bible for many years, I can tell you that even many believers don't *really* buy into this story. It is Sunday school 101 type of material—everyone is told about the Tower of Babel. We pay homage to this tale, and pretend that God actually transported everyone around the world and changed their languages. But the number of professed Christians who take this idea seriously is far fewer than the number who know the story, believe me. In truth, I failed to take this account as sincere truth throughout much of my life. Sure, something happened at Babel, but it must be deeply metaphorical. This was just their way of generally saying that people came to inhabit the whole Earth, and that many languages came about in human history.

What I came to understand is what I believe we all should: the Bible is not joking about the events at Babel. When it repeatedly says that God scattered the people "across the earth," it means just that. This view may fall under the dreaded "literal interpretation" category, but it seems wholly appropriate at times, and this is one of them. Like the Flood, we have another place where the stories of prominent ancient peoples and the biblical narrative find common ground. The best we can tell—aside from the endless scientific hypotheses that can be conjured, and are ever-changing—is that the world was host to many different civilizations of people, who spoke diverse languages, at a very early time. This is so much the case that we cannot tell with any certainty which group came first.

Perhaps this is because they all came about at roughly the same time. Maybe there really was a great scattering of people, and a great confusion of languages, at one point in human history. No one is claiming that cultures did not traverse the world on their own, via ships or possibly even by crossing long-buried land bridges. These things no doubt happened to some degree, but they probably happened *after* groups were already scattered around the world. As I previously said, no ancient civilization just started out with the types of vessels needed to cross the oceans (unless that technology was given to them). There are also the issues of how they would have done so without maps, how they would have accomplished mass migrations at great speeds, and how they developed their many languages so quickly. In all, it seems as though a Babel-type event was necessary, and all of the corroborating evidence supports this idea. As strange as it may seem, even to the Bible-believers among us, it really happened.

Chapter Three
Too Strange for Fiction

Ever since it first aired in 2009, I have been utterly fascinated by the show *River Monsters*. Though it is no longer running—and has been replaced with other shows, like *Jeremy Wade's Mighty Rivers*—the concept still peaks my interest. There are a few major reasons for this. The first is that I come from a long family of fishermen, and I enjoy catching the whiskered predators of the night—catfish, for the uninitiated—more than just about any other leisure activity there is. The second reason is that the show is built around investigating many of the myths and legends surrounding giant and/or dangerous aquatic creatures.

Jeremy Wade was not just the star of the show; he is a well-educated, intelligent man, who also happens to be extremely reasonable. Wade has been studying monster fish—and the legends behind them—for more than thirty years. He has heard almost every crazy story out there about man-eating sea creatures, and he has caught specimens that most of us would never even believe existed. With all of his experience chasing these mysteries, Jeremy Wade always reminds his audience of something very important: no matter how fantastic a story may sound, there is usually some degree of truth to it. In fact, the truth behind the legend is sometimes even stranger than the legend itself.

I think this same line of reasoning should be applied to the "myths" and "legends" of the ancient peoples. More than that, we should also acknowledge that the same is true for many of life's unexplainable mysteries. While it is accurate that any story can ultimately become outlandish, there is more often than not a great deal of truth involved in even the most incredible claims. Occasionally, as the old saying goes, truth can be stranger than fiction. I believe that there are a number of very odd occurrences that precisely fit into this category. When investigated, I also believe they can provide further reasons—if only circumstantial in nature—to believe that there are higher powers at work in our world. There are extraterrestrials, in the truest sense of the word.

A Combustible Relationship

Frank Baker is not exactly a household name. The vast majority of people living on planet Earth have probably never heard of him. Odds are that you have never heard of him, either. Frank is one of a number of people throughout history who have experienced something truly bizarre—spontaneous human combustion (SHC). In essence, SHC is an event in which a human being initiates a fire on his or her person, without the application of heat from an external source; nothing can be pinpointed as the cause, so the fire appears to have originated on or within the individual. Frank Baker's alleged cases of SHC have been documented for some time now, appearing everywhere from local news stations to the Science Channel's *The Unexplained Files*.[80] On two separate occasions, Frank claims to have simply burst into flames out of nowhere: not once, but twice. Frank recalled the following about the first event: "We were getting ready for fishing and sitting on the couch . . . Everything was great. Pete was sitting next to me [and] we were having a helluva time."[81] In the midst of all the fun, Frank proceeded to burst into flames.

A fantastic claim, certainly, but he was not alone either of the times this supposedly occurred. Baker's good friend, Pete Willey, was present on both of these occasions. Willey summarized the events in his own unique way: "It was the damndest thing I've ever seen . . . Frank was freaking out and making me freak out."[82] Fortunately, Willey was able to dampen the flames and Frank escaped with only burns to his arms. When Frank went to the doctor, he claimed that the medical professional who

---

[80] See "Human Combustion Victim."
[81] See David Moye's article, "Frank Baker Discusses Spontaneous Combustion Experience On 'The Unexplained Files'."
[82] Ibid.

evaluated him felt as though the flames had come from within his body; there was no external cause.

While mystifying, Frank Baker's experiences are by no stretch the only examples of spontaneous human combustion. In July of 1951, Mary Hardy Reeser—known to some as "The Cinder Lady"—is believed by many to have burst into flames in her apartment. As is often the case (for some reason), certain body parts were unaffected, even though others had been utterly destroyed; one foot remained intact, as well as her shrunken skull (odd). John Irving Bentley (1966) and Henry Thomas (1980) were also found incinerated, though both retained at least one leg. Strangely enough, the slipper covering Bentley's remaining foot was completely untouched.[83] The fire really had consumed him, and him alone.

One of the most famous cases of SHC, and one of the most recent, was the strange case of Michael Faherty. Faherty was discovered on December 22, 2010, in his home in Ballybane, Ireland. According to reports, only Faherty's body, as well as the areas *directly* above and below him, were affected by the flames. The coroner on the case actually felt as though spontaneous human combustion was the most reasonable explanation for the event.[84] These are just a few of the more notable cases throughout history. The N.F.P.A. (National Fire Protection Association) suggests that either spontaneous combustion or chemical reaction accounted for an average of 14,070 fires *per year* between 2005 and 2009, more than half of which were actually residential fires.[85] Residential fires—the exact locations described in the above cases of SHC. But there is a profound difference: none of those cases involved people being turned to ash, with almost no other damage to their surroundings.

What can we make of spontaneous human combustion? Certainly, many dispute the particulars of these cases, but we have a few basic options at our disposal. First, we could simply choose to ignore these

---

[83] Andrew Handley, "Top 10 Unsolved Cases of Spontaneous Human Combustion."
[84] Ibid.
[85] Ben Evarts, "Spontaneous combustion or chemical reaction."

incidents altogether, chalking them up to some sort of science fiction mumbo jumbo. That is easy enough to do, but it is also dishonest and contrary to the evidence. Second, we could assume that there must be some completely "rational," naturalistic explanation for these events. This seems to be the standard approach to strange cases of all varieties.

While we have absolutely no idea how a human body could burn to ash—exceeding 3,000 degrees Fahrenheit in the process—without so much as setting fire to the items around them, we could still postulate that we will *someday* uncover an explanation that will of course be devoid of any and all metaphysical implications. This is called "wishing on the future." If you are unfamiliar with this concept, simply consult any number of our contemporary high school or college biology textbooks. These typically ensure students that, despite the innumerable problems with Darwinism (or the "neo-Darwinian Synthesis") and other evolutionary theories, we *will* fill in all the gaps at some point in the future. It seems that no one is able to ridicule the concept of faith, while employing so much of it within their own fields of study, quite like the good people working in the biological sciences. That, of course, applies only to those within the mainstream, and not to every person.

There is a third option though. Instead of sweeping the issue under the rug or negating the possibility of metaphysical intervention in principle, we could at least permit that examples of spontaneous human combustion are best explained as acts performed by powerful, non-human entities. If we were to consider this notion, what type of entities would we be talking about? There are a few possibilities here as well, but two primary options: foreign beings from somewhere else in the universe, or beings from some other realm of existence. That is, the aliens of ancient astronaut theory, or the heavenly beings of the Bible and certain other religious texts. Both would have to be capable of startling displays of power, and both get to the heart of the angel-alien debate. Certainly, it has been posited that aliens are responsible for the known cases of SHC. In this context, "aliens" are intended to be understood as beings that exist within the known universe, who have literally ventured from their place in the cosmos to our planet.

Presumably, these beings arrive here via their advanced flying crafts, and they proceed to fry human beings into ashes upon arrival. As mentioned at the onset of the book, the notion that UFOs—and therefore, the existence of other intelligent beings within our universe—exist is difficult to reject. But would *that type* of "extraterrestrial" make sense of SHC? I don't believe so. There are no known cases (so far as I am aware) of SHC that are in any way linked to the appearance of flying crafts or strange sightings. If an alien being were to make an interstellar voyage to our Earth and dissolve a human being into ashes, surely *someone* would have seen *something*. There is also the arbitrary nature of such an event. Why would an alien from another planet go through such efforts to kill someone on Earth whom they had no real way of knowing, and why would it make sure that there was no trace of its presence left behind? If the point was to show its incredible power, leaving no trace would defeat the purpose. Maybe they just do it for sport, like the hunters on the movie *Predator*. I suppose anything is technically possible, but that sure doesn't sound very realistic.

If there doesn't appear to be any indication that beings from another part of the universe are to blame for these bizarre events, what type of entities could be responsible? A crucial element to remember about the nature of SHC cases is that the victims essentially appear to be "zapped" into ash *out of nowhere*. Despite the push for various "wick theories"—which generally posit that the human body is something like a candle wick that slowly burns, as subcutaneous fat is released from the body—there simply has been no satisfying naturalistic explanation for the cases of SHC. This is largely because the victims are generally turned to dust, while most everything around them remains unchanged.

As previously mentioned, even the soft fabrics around them are often completely untouched, and there is never an indication that anyone else—a human being or an extraterrestrial being—was physically present at all. For all intents and purposes, only the person is destroyed: and destroyed quickly, it appears. Only the person is the target. Bear in mind that this is something we even have a difficult time doing to bodies. Even after burning a corpse for hours, at heats in excess of 1,100 degrees Fahrenheit, crematoriums typically have to grind up the remaining bones.[86] So, where does that leave us? In all likelihood, it leaves us with beings from another realm. It leaves us with beings that do not have to cross galaxies in a spaceship, but are simply able to interact with our world by crossing a realm or a dimension. This would be an entity that could remain both completely unseen by the naked eye and leave no trace of its presence. We would have to be talking about something like a god, an angel, or perhaps even a demon.

At this point, it would be easy enough to close the book and believe that I am "out to lunch" on all of this. This is particularly true if you are a Christian or someone of another religious tradition. In truth, there was probably a time when I would have felt the same way. But would it shock you if I said that the Bible actually supports the possibility that beings from another realm can cause something like SHC? Yes, *we already believe this.*

Who among us can forget the mystifying story of Uzzah and the Ark of the Covenant? As recorded in the book of Exodus, the Israelites were commanded to construct a transportable vessel that would ultimately house the presence of their God, Yahweh. By virtue of God's presence with the Ark, it was an extraordinarily powerful relic. It was also incredibly dangerous for those who had to carry it. God gave the command that only particular Levites (the consecrated priests) should carry the Ark of the Covenant (Num. 7:9), and that they must carry the Ark by its specially designed poles (Ex. 25:12-14). But what if an ark-bearer should have to reach down and grab this relic, in order to keep it from falling to the ground?

---

[86] Michelle Kim, "How Cremation Works."

Poor Uzzah discovered the answer to this question the hard way. The Bible records the event as follows: ". . . Uzzah reached out and took hold of the ark of God, because the oxen stumbled. The Lord's anger burned against Uzzah because of his irreverent act; therefore God struck him down, and he died there beside the ark of God."[87] Clearly, the text does not say that Uzzah was incinerated, but it does tell us that God is capable of causing spontaneous death to individuals. We actually see this in the New Testament as well, when two persons named Ananias and Sapphira were struck down on the spot for withholding money from the church and lying about it (Acts 5:1-11). While Uzzah may not fit the precise description of SHC, this does tell us that otherrealmly beings are capable of destroying humans on the spot. It also causes us to wonder if there may not be other biblical examples that more closely match the cases of SHC.

It is often thought that the first cases of SHC date to the 17th century AD,[88] but that may well be nearly three millennia off the mark. It was one bad day for the cities of Sodom and Gomorrah, to say the least. After Abraham had spent time in a series of negotiations with God—with the hopes of keeping God from destroying two of the most godless and immoral cities in history—fire and brimstone poured from the sky, and everyone living within these cities was utterly incinerated. But those weren't the only casualties that day.

There is one other of serious note, and serious obscurity. Just prior to destroying the cities of Sodom and Gomorrah, a man named Lot—the nephew of the famous Old Testament Patriarch, Abraham—was told to take his family and flee to a small town called Zoar, in order to escape the coming catastrophe (Gen. 19:21-22). There was one catch, however. The two angels who had been staying with Lot's family instructed them to flee quickly, *without pausing to look back* at the destruction. As with most of the commands given to God's people throughout the Old Testament, it

---

[87] 2 Samuel 6:6-7.
[88] History.com, "Is spontaneous human combustion real?"

was not followed to the letter. Genesis records that Lot's wife stopped to look back, the result being that she was turned into a "pillar of salt" (Gen. 19:26).

The question here is whether or not Lot's wife was literally turned into one the world's most primitive food seasonings/preservatives. Transliterated, the Hebrew word adapted here is *melach*, and it does equate to the term "salt." But few interpreters believe that God literally turned Lot's wife directly into a pillar of salt, even though salt deposits are quite common in many of the regions near the Dead Sea (close to where this would have taken place). Rather, it is often suggested that her desire to maintain her previous life in Sodom caused her to lag behind, ultimately forcing her to become party to those who were being destroyed.[89]

Perhaps she was covered by the explosions of surrounding salt deposits, or maybe she was ultimately petrified (becoming "salt") under piles of ash.[90] Whatever the case, it is important to consider the context of the situation. God—a non-human, metaphysical being—caused a fire and a heat of such magnitude that the cities of Sodom and Gomorrah (and their inhabitants) were absolutely obliterated. So was Lot's wife. Being turned into an ash-statue in a flash is pretty similar to what we see in cases of SHC. It's hard to ignore the commonalties.

So, we have established that the God of the Bible can (and has) caused the immediate death of individuals, and that He is able to do so via fiery catastrophes. That is, if you believe in these accounts (which I do). But can we get any closer to the type of powers displayed in cases of SHC? Actually, we can. When I first started considering these issues, one biblical text immediately came to mind: Leviticus 9:24. Leviticus, being aptly named for the tribe of Levi, is a text that has a great deal to do with the priestly requirements within the ancient Israelite community. In particular, the sacrificial system and the dire seriousness of sin come to the forefront. After Moses' brother, Aaron, and the Levites had been

---

[89] Henry M. Morris. *The Genesis Record,* 355-356.
[90] Ibid.

inaugurated as the priests of Israel, God ordered that a series of sacrifices be made. One of the sacrifices was to be a "burnt offering," which consisted of both a calf and a lamb (9:3).

After making all of the appropriate sacrifices and placing both the burnt offering and fat portions on the altar, something astonishing happened: "Fire came out from the presence of the Lord and consumed the burnt offering and the fat portions on the altar. And when all the people saw it, they shouted for joy and fell face down" (9:24). In an instant, *fire consumed* the parts. This isn't the only time something like this happened in the Old Testament, either. In his spiritual battle with the prophets of the god Baal, Elijah called upon Yahweh to demonstrate His superiority—and He did. Two bulls were sacrificed and set on altars to test the competing deities. The contest was simple: whichever god sent fire to burn the sacrifices was the *real* God. Where the 450 prophets of Baal had failed, Elijah succeeded. It is said that Yahweh sent fire to swallow up the bull that had been sacrificed: a fire so intense that it destroyed the entire altar, and even ". . . licked up the water in the trench" that surrounded it (1 Ki. 18:38). Just think—a fire so intense that it even caused the surrounding water to immediately dissipate.

Pardon the obvious pun, but we may be getting warmer. Perhaps God (or angelic beings) is the most likely explanation for the cases of SHC. But wait a minute; not so fast. In the book of Job—which, depending on whatever date one goes with, could potentially be the oldest book in the entire Bible—we see another being that is said to be responsible for astonishing displays of blazing destruction. After accusing the stunningly righteous Job of serving God for entirely selfish purposes, Satan—meaning literally, "the accuser"—negotiates a deal with God. If God permits Satan to make Job's life into a living hell, Job would undoubtedly abandon his faith and curse his Maker.

God clearly doesn't buy into this idea, and is willing to allow Satan to fail with his hypothesis. On route to destroying just about everything and everyone that Job held dear, the Bible records that Satan was able to conjure one truly hellacious firestorm. In true Sodom and Gomorrah fashion, Satan poured fire from the heavens, completely eradicating all of Job's sheep and his servants (1:16). While the book of Job clearly displays many metaphorical features—his perfect numbers of animals (7,000 and 3,000) and children (seven sons and three daughters) being obvious examples—the Bible is clear throughout that Satan is a being of great power. Even in the New Testament, Satan is given aliases like the "god of this age" (2 Cor. 4:4) and the "prince of the power of the air" (Eph. 2:2). Clearly, producing fiery death and destruction is not outside the realm of his abilities, or his desires.

While none of this *perfectly* equates to the cases of SHC, it is clear that the Bible presents us with beings that can cause both sudden death and incineration. If God can cause fire to rain down and devour entire cities, turn people into ash, and completely consume offerings (even the water that surrounds them) in an instant, it is no stretch to say that the God of the Bible could cause SHC in His sleep. This could also be said of Satan, and conceivably other demonic entities. Am I saying that Yahweh was responsible for catching Frank Baker on fire and for destroying people like Michael Faherty? Personally, I doubt it. Never once does the Bible describe God as an arbitrary distributor of destruction; as far as the Bible is concerned, God is always said to be responding to human disobedience and sin when that kind of destruction is involved.

Satan, on the other hand, is always described as being an adversary to the righteous; he would want to do such things. Does that mean Satan is responsible and God is not? In truth, I simply don't know. What I do know is that non-human, metaphysical beings like God, Satan, and the angels are as good an explanation for the cases of SHC as anything else. In my mind, they are much better explanations. I also know that the Bible actually describes many instances where similar things have happened.

Finally, I believe that these otherrealmly beings are *much* more plausible explanations for SHC than are beings that fly across the galaxy, in order to set people on fire. A being from another realm could potentially incinerate someone without the least bit of detection; they could simply step right into our world, at will. Alternatively, a being coming here from somewhere in the universe would undoubtedly leave some sign of its presence. Moreover, an entity from another realm could also monitor us and our behavior at all times, because there would be no spatial separation: no distance. On the other hand, a being from another planet would have to be physically present—and thus, detectible—in order to do so. If extraterrestrials are responsible for SHC, then we would probably do well to consider God and the angelic beings as the extraterrestrials.

Strength in Numbers

What I am about to discuss as evidence of extraterrestrial beings (broadly speaking) has been cited as an oddity within our world and universe for a very long time. Many of Earth's greatest structures are laden with the repetition of specific numbers, as is the "language of the universe:" mathematics. The strange recurrence of particular numbers within human history and the mathematics ingrained in the cosmos is often cited as evidence for beings from another planet, but it is also used to suggest the very existence of a Creator God.

Here, again, we must distinguish between beings who literally live somewhere within our universe and beings who live within an entirely different realm, one that is spatially or dimensionally separate from our own. But which type of being would make the best sense of the inexplicable connection between abstract objects like numbers and our material world? If numbers are indeed evidence of extraterrestrial intelligence, what type of intelligence are they proof of? These are precisely the questions taken up in this particular section of the book.

The two primary numbers that come to the forefront of this discussion should sound extremely familiar to anyone who has even a basic understanding of the Bible. I am referring, of course, to the numbers three and seven. Specifically, the number three has incredible importance with regards to the topics involved in this book. While I will be spending more time discussing the number three, I do at least want to mention some of the profound ways that the number seven shows up in our world, and in varying religious perspectives. First, let's notice some obvious—and some that are not so obvious—examples.

Have you noticed that there are seven continents on planet Earth? What about the fact that there are Seven Wonders of the World? You probably have noticed this. Pretty basic, I know. There are also seven Wonders of the Ancient World, seven Natural Wonders of the World, and other lists of seven "wonders." There are seven days in a week. There are seven "deadly sins," seven main colors of a rainbow, seven seas (or oceanic bodies), seven Classical Planets, and seven Metals of Antiquity, from which the modern world was formed. In mathematics, seven is a prime number, a Mersenne prime, and even a double Mersenne prime (very rare). There are seven "frieze groups," seven fundamental types of "catastrophes," and all manner of other incredibly complex sevens in mathematics.[91] All of this is just a tiny sampling of the ways that the number seven is written into the core of human existence.

In more modern times, we can see that there are seven numbers that comprise a phone number. There are two primary reasons for this. The first is that seven digits was a logical step from the previous four-digit number sequence, because it allowed a much greater range of combinations, as more and more people began to use a telephone.[92] Eventually, seven was not enough, so a three-digit area code was added to the front of each phone number. Imagine that: three plus seven.

But there is a more intriguing reason why seven is a suitable figure for something like a telephone number. It turns out that countless studies

---

[91] See the *Wikipedia* article, "7", for many more ways the number seven comes up in mathematics.
[92] See the Allconnect article, "Why We Use 7 Digits and Other Fun Phone Facts."

have shown that the longest sequence of numbers that most of us can recall at the spur of the moment is seven. When psychologist George Miller made this discovery 1956, he dubbed this limit the "magical number seven."[93] This corresponds with the reality that the brain's short-term memory can hold about seven chunks of information.[94] In the brain, seven truly appears to be a "magic number."[95] The number seven is built into the way our brains function.

Turning to ancient religious traditions, it is well-established that the number seven has extraordinary importance within the Bible. Seven is the number of completion: of utter perfection, even. God created the heavens and the earth in seven total days, with the seventh day being a crucial part of the process because it announced completion. Joshua and the Israelites paraded around Jericho for seven days, in order to bring about its demise (Jos. 6).

In the New Testament, Jesus instructs his followers to forgive others "seventy times seven" times (Mt. 18:22). In the Gospel of John, Jesus provides his observers with seven "signs" and seven accompanying "discourses" (Jn. 1:19-11:57). The book of Revelation describes seven trumpets, seven bowls of wrath, and seven seals.[96] Just this brief focus on the number seven reveals that there is something very unique about it. For whatever reason, it is a number that some higher intelligence clearly wants human beings to identify with. With these basic associations in place, it is time to move on to the number three.

The Egyptian pyramids were previously mentioned because of their incredible engineering complexity, but what should also be pointed out is the simpler fact that there are three prominent pyramids at Giza. There is the Great Pyramid (Khufu), which of course receives the most

---

[93] Ibid.
[94] Ibid.
[95] See Schenkman's article, "In the Brain, Seven is a Magic Number" for more on this phenomenon.
[96] See Revelation, cc. 5-8, 8-11, and 16 for these events.

recognition, but Khufu is accompanied by Khafre (the second largest) and Menkaure (the smallest). It is no matter of sheer happenstance that the pyramids at Giza also appear to align with Orion's Belt, of the Orion constellation. We have three prominent structures that match up with three prominent stars. There are many surrounding stars, so why just those?

Far from Egypt, there is another set of pyramids that share all of the same qualities. Arial photographs of China's Great Pyramids of Xi'an, as well as Mexico's Great Pyramids of Teotihuacan, show a remarkable—more like identical, really—arrangement.[97] Naturally, both of these sets of pyramids also align with Orion's Belt. Neolithic monuments like the famous Stonehenge and the *three*-stoned monument known as "Avebury" even exhibit triangular patterns. Wherever we find written records from the various ancient cultures, we find that the builders of these amazing structures were quite insistent about whom they had received their technological, mathematical, and astrological understandings from: the gods, or the higher beings.

This mentioning of the "gods" leads us quite naturally into other places where the number three has been mysteriously prominent in historical thought. Being aggressively polytheistic (believing in multiple deities), the Greeks had a great many gods who were each considered to control certain aspects of human life. The Olympian god Hermes was thought to be the son of the leader of the gods, Zeus, and the goddess Maia. Having been spawned by Zeus himself, Hermes' place in the Greek pantheon was quite important.

Hermes was responsible for anything from mediating between human beings, to safe travel, to athletics, to escorting souls to the Greek underworld (Hades), and many other things. For our purposes, one of the more interesting aspects of the god Hermes is his relationship to the number three. Based on his role as both an intermediate between the

---

[97] "Ancient Pyramids Match the Alignment of Orion's Belt."

realm of the gods and an escort for human souls into the underworld, Hermes is essentially the god connected to the three great realms: the realm of the gods, the realm of humanity, and the realm of the dead.

There is also another Hermes in later Greek thought who is sometimes (probably errantly) connected to the son of Zeus, and he is known as Hermes Trismegistus. In simpler terms, this name meant "Thrice Great Hermes." The *Corpus Hermeticum*—a mysterious collection of writings largely focusing on philosophical and theological ideas—was attributed to Hermes Trismegistus. Because of its discussion of the three united fields of astrology, alchemy, and magic, the *Corpus Hermeticum* ignited a great deal of interest in these practices during the Renaissance, after it had been translated into Latin.[98] It is thought that it was Hermes Trimegistus' ability to be a human conduit for divine intelligence, and his ability to put this information into written form, that lead to his title of "thrice great."[99]

If we look to the Hindu faith, we also see a very obvious connection to the number three. The three *chief* deities—collectively known as the "Trimurti," or the three forms of God—are Brahma, Vishnu, and Shiva. In some sense, one could see these deities as the Hindu Trinity. In a basic way, this triad of gods is in charge of creating (Brahma), preserving (Vishnu), and even destroying and/or transforming (Shiva). In Christian thought, do we not generally regard the Father as the Creator, the Son as the preserver or sustainer, and the Spirit as the transformer? The overlap is clearly not a perfect one, but there is an undeniable similarity.

Interestingly, Shiva is often depicted as carrying a trident (a three-pronged spear) that is roughly supposed to represent Shiva's three essential powers of will, action, and knowledge. Stranger than that, Shiva is also frequently portrayed on various monuments or writings as possessing a third eye. With this third eye, Shiva is thought to be able to see the plane of higher consciousness: the realm of the divine. In all, Hinduism presents us with three

---

[98] Christopher Warnock, "Hermes Trismegistus: Hermetic Philosophy, Astrology & Magic."
[99] Ibid.

chief forms of God, one of them possessing both a trident of power and a third eye.

Mahāyāna Buddhism—the most prominent branch of Buddhism of the present day—also promotes the notion that there are three divine powers at play in existence. The Mahāyāna Buddhism writings often describe a buddha named Amitābha, meaning "infinite light." While Amitābha is sometimes pictured alone in Buddhist imagery, he is also frequently depicted with two helpers or assistants, named Avalokiteśvara and Mahāsthāmaprāpta. Accordingly, these three beings generate somewhat of a trinity, loosely uniting the various forms of Buddhism. Interestingly, Mahāsthāmaprāpta is considered to be the embodiment of wisdom. To think, part of the triad from an eastern religion being referred to as the embodiment of wisdom! Who could forget Paul's words in 1 Corinthians 1:22-24?

> "For indeed Jews ask for signs and Greeks search for wisdom; but we preach Christ crucified, to Jews a stumbling block and to Gentiles foolishness, but to those who are the called, both Jews and Greeks, Christ the power of God and the wisdom of God."

Wisdom personified—which is a theme going back to the "Lady Wisdom" figure found within the wisdom and poetry section of the Old Testament (particularly Proverbs)—finally became *literally* embodied: Jesus was wisdom incarnate.

Certainly, there is a powerful connection between the number three and the most prominent religions of the world. I probably don't need to say it, but I'm going to anyway: as Christians, *we already believe* in this connection. Noah had three sons (Gen. 6:10), and Job had three daughters (1:2). There were three sacred elements—a jar of manna, Aaron's staff, and the tablets inscribed with the Ten Commandments—stored within the Ark of the Covenant (Heb. 9:4). Jonah famously stayed within the belly of the great fish for three full days (1:17). Jesus was given three temptations in the wilderness (Mat. 4:1-11), and he called three disciples to be part of his "inner circle" (John, James, and Peter). Jesus rose from the dead after three days (1 Cor. 15:4). Peter denied Jesus three times (Lk. 22:54-62), and Jesus later questioned Peter three times in accordance with the betrayal (Jn. 21:15-17).

In the book of Revelation, there are essentially three evil entities (or the "unholy trinity," as they are sometimes called) in association with the forces of evil: the Dragon, the Beast, and the False Prophet. Then there is the most obvious three of all—the Trinity, or Godhead. This theme is seen all over the Bible, from the plural "let us" statements of Genesis to the clear designation of the Father, the Son, and the Holy Spirit at both the baptism of Jesus (Mat. 3:13-17) and the Great Commission (Mat. 28:18-20). These are just a few—really, just the tip of the iceberg—of the various connections the Bible shares with the number three, but it should be enough to make the point.

With the overabundance of threes contained within the architecture of the ancients and the greatest religions of the world, it would be sheer ludicrous to chalk all of this up to chance. Surely, these examples (and many others) cannot just be excused as a giant case of apophenia: seeing or perceiving connections between things when there are none. But we still have the question: which type of beings can best explain the connection between numbers and our world? Are the "gods" of Buddhism and Hinduism, and the three persons of the Trinity in Christianity, actually aliens that descended from somewhere else in the universe, or are they actually divine beings from another realm? In answering that question, we should first briefly consider the nature of numbers.

Properly understood, numbers are abstract objects. That is, numbers are not physically found in our material world. Like thoughts and ideas, numbers cannot be touched. For all intents and purposes, they are proven real to us because they *correspond with* material realities. As I have written elsewhere, you cannot have a negative number of anything—say, -2 apples—in reality.[100] Yet, for some strange reason, these abstract realities we call "numbers" explain much of what we actually do see and experience in our material world. Numbers are not reducible to naturalistic explanation, yet they do explain the natural world. Numbers can be odd things indeed. Pun intended.

In creating the pyramids, the Egyptians utilized mathematical principles that would later be *officially* espoused by a brilliant Greek man named Pythagoras. While it has perhaps been a very long time for most of you who are reading this book (as it had been for me), you may remember something called the "Pythagorean Theorem" from junior high or high school math classes. The equation is so simple, yet so profound: $a^2 + b^2 = c^2$. That is, the square of the hypotenuse—which is the long side of a right triangle, directly opposite of the right angle—equals the sum of the squares of the other two sides. The equation is straightforward, but is anything but simple to understand. More than that, imagine trying to first discover this principle. That is no easy task, to say the least.

It seems to be quite a stretch to say that we could have discovered this type of information entirely on our own and without assistance. I mean, cultures were employing this understanding long before the time of Pythagoras. But for the sake of discussion, let's momentarily grant that the human race has never had any help with advanced mathematical understandings, such as the principles behind the Pythagorean Theorem. The much bigger issue concerns what type of beings could *create* mathematical relationships and abstract objects, like numbers. It is one thing to discover them, but it is quite another thing to produce them.

It is one thing to observe and extrapolate the information involved in functional equations like $a^2 + b^2 = c^2$, but it is an entirely different thing to create the circumstances that make the Pythagorean Theorem (and countless others) a valid description of how the material world actually functions. As with most

---

[100] In *Mind Over Matter: The Necessity of Metaphysics in a Material World*, we discuss the reality that the very fact that numbers correspond with reality is substantial in proving the existence of God. See pages 72-76, in particular.

things, there is a clear difference between *observing* how something works, and *creating* that something to work. We can all see how something like a trebuchet operates, but how many of us could walk out and construct one on our own, without any type of help or guidance? This problem would be compounded, if we had never even heard of a trebuchet. The cultures that first understood advanced mathematical principles had no *earthly* examples to draw from.

I could have discussed many other ways that the numbers three and seven permeate almost every part of our lives and our history, but these examples should suffice. It is perfectly reasonable that there could be beings of higher intelligence that exist elsewhere in the universe, and that they could have related the incredible nature of mathematics and the power of certain numbers to us earthlings. In the most common sense of the word, these types of "aliens" could have done this much. The problem is that these types of beings—no matter how intellectually advanced they might be—could never be responsible for creating numbers, or the way in which they combine to explain the inner workings of the universe.

At what point does a race of beings become so sophisticated that they can create something like gravitational laws or mathematical constants? As we will later see with Jesus' astonishing miracles, simply being "smarter" than us is not enough. Creating mathematical relationships of this sort is not simply a matter of sheer intelligence (though it certainly includes it), but a matter of simultaneously possessing unimaginable power. It seems that we might again be talking about something more like God or angelic beings than a group of hyper-intelligent entities from another planet. Even if the latter shared knowledge with us, they too would be subject to those laws and constants.

Dark Forces

In March of 2012, Dr. Richard E. Gallagher—of the New York Medical College—released a report that no doubt raised eyebrows among his esteemed colleagues. In this report, a woman named "Julia" (a pseudonym used to protect her identity) was alleged to have been possessed by an unseen force. Julia was described as entering into insane trances, speaking in very dark tones and in languages she had never previously studied, exhibiting a supernatural understanding about the people working on her case, and at one point, she even supposedly levitated six inches in the air for around thirty minutes.[101] This type of account could surprise some readers, but might be perfectly believable to others. This would certainly depend upon our various worldviews.

As with any claim of this kind, there has been no shortage of pushback. I recall a series of letters to the editor that were published in *The Washington Post*. The article title is a dead giveaway of what we can expect to find in its contents: "The self-possessed psychiatrist Richard Gallagher should exorcise his delusions."[102] Not only is Gallagher himself apparently delusional and self-possessed, he also—as one letter said— "overlooked myriad alternate (non-'demonic') scenarios that might fully account for the phenomena he observed." In other words, as long as there are other *possible* naturalistic explanations for something, it is irresponsible to invoke paranormal or supernatural intervention. Where have we heard that reasoning before?

Another letter stated that this account was just another "god of the gaps" situation: a place where "supernatural stories are used to fill in what science has not yet explained." This is a favorite (and a completely debunked)[103] argument that scientific and philosophical materialists love to use against anything that remotely smells of divine intervention. We are told that science will someday explain everything in the biological world (and all other things, of course), so to invoke a being of higher power is to place a false plug into the temporary "gap." Maybe one day we will hear

---

[101] Adrian Asis, "6 Cases of 'Demonic Possession' That Might Convince You."
[102] *The Washington Post*, "The self-possessed psychiatrist Richard Gallagher should exorcise his delusions."
[103] I dealt with this objection in *Mind Over Matter: The Necessity of Metaphysics in a Material World*, 15-22. This argument has also been destroyed by many other thinkers, but persists nonetheless.

something that resembles a fresh argument from the skeptical crowd. Here's to hoping!

Whether we believe Gallagher's account or not, this story gets us thinking about another peculiar aspect of reality: one that strikes at the heart of the discussion about extraterrestrial beings, and the role that dark forces might play in our world. Indeed, it is difficult to find a culture or a religion that does not assert that some type of malevolent entity (or entities) exists, and that this force can negatively affect human beings. If true, could this tell us something about the nature of beings that are more ancient, more intelligent, and more powerful than we are?

Would pinpointing the identities of the forces that have set themselves against humanity actually give us a better idea about whether we are dealing with beings from another planet or beings from an entirely different realm or dimension? Like the previous topics, I believe that it can. In fact, I believe that the evidence for dark entities—and their attacks on humanity—is some of the most important when discussing the existence of extraterrestrial powers.

Nearly every notable religion in history has made space for the role that evil entities play within our existence. The Persian religion, Zoroastrianism, contained a group of foul beings called the *daeva*s, which were essentially considered to be adversaries of the "One Wise Lord" Ahura Mazda and his creation. There is also the notion of an ultimate evil entity within Zoroastrianism, which is the Evil Spirit Ahriman. Further, there were good beings named *ahuras*, which are eerily similar to the angelic beings discussed within the Bible. Hindu belief regarded the counterpart of the *ahuras*—who are known as the *asuras*—as evil entities that resemble what the Bible describes as demons.[104]

The Egyptians believed in an evil god named Set who fell from the grace of the pantheon after murdering his brother. They also believed in demonic activity. For example, the demon Nehebkau—who was

---

[104] Linwood Fredericksen, "Angel and Demon."

sometimes regarded as an earth spirit and a source of strength for the other gods—was often viewed as being a menacing monster: a sort of serpent/human hybrid who could affect the souls of the dead.[105] Sounds a bit familiar, doesn't it? Islam affirms the existence of the Devil (called Iblis, or Shaitan). He is thought to command the darker group of beings called "shaitans," who belong to a class of supernatural forces called djinni or jinni (*genies*, to you and me).[106]

While some of these notions about malevolent beings and their impact in our world may strain credibility to many Christians, we have to ask ourselves if our own beliefs are so very different. I feel as though they are not so dissimilar at all. In fact, I think that the Bible's portrayal of demonic beings is perhaps even more extraordinary than most that were previously discussed. Now don't get me wrong: "extraordinary" should not be equated with terms like "absurd" or "ridiculous." I am simply saying that as Christians, *we already believe* that incredible events have (and do) transpire between good beings and evil beings. We call these entities "angels" and "demons." Though everyone has heard of these powers, it would surprise most of us to know that the New Testament is chock-full of descriptions about them. To see this point, let us first look at Christianity's central figure—Jesus of Nazareth.

To say that Jesus was *just an exorcist* is sort of like saying Jerry Rice was just a wide receiver, or Isaac Newton was just a physicist. All three of these people certainly were an exorcist, a wide receiver, and a physicist, respectively. But anyone who knows much about them understands that they were more like the embodiment of those professions. Jerry Rice is still the best receiver in NFL history. Isaac Newton is regarded as being the father of modern physics (if not the most intelligent scientist in all of history).

Jesus was the exorcist of all exorcists. It takes no time flat to begin seeing this reality within the New Testament. In the Gospel of Mark—

---

[105] "Devils and Demons."
[106] Ibid.

which has long been thought of as the first gospel account to be written—Jesus' very first miracle came in the form of an exorcism. Mark 1:23-26 records the following:

> "Just then there was a man in their synagogue with an unclean spirit; and he cried out, saying, 'What business do we have with each other, Jesus of Nazareth? Have You come to destroy us? I know who You are—the Holy One of God!' And Jesus rebuked him, saying, 'Be quiet, and come out of him!' Throwing him into convulsions, the unclean spirit cried out with a loud voice and came out of him."

Not only was this Jesus' first miracle (at least within Mark), it was also the event that lead to his initial popularity. The Gospel later records that the people who witnessed this event were so astonished that Jesus' fame spread across the entire region of Galilee afterwards (1:28). According to Mark, the "whole town" gathered around Simon Peter's house so they could either be healed of a disease or delivered from demonic possession (1:33-34). Let's face it: much of Jesus' early fame was the direct result of his abilities as an exorcist.

From there, the gospels go on to collectively attest to many confrontations between Jesus and evil spirits. The Gospel of Luke records Jesus' run-in with a collection of demons who had obtained possession over a man (4:31-35). As usual, the people were absolutely astounded by his ability to deliver the man from the demons, and his fame continued to spread (4:37). Immediately after that, scores of people came to Jesus for relief from their demonic oppression (Lk. 4:41). Mark 9:14-29 records that Jesus even liberated a possessed boy from a demon who was literally trying to kill him.

Matthew 15:21-28 tells of a similar encounter that Jesus had with a demon, but this time it was a young girl who was miraculously healed of her possession. Amazingly, sometimes Jesus himself was accused of being demon-possessed because of the incredible power he displayed during his many exorcisms![107] Jesus even commissioned and empowered his disciples to perform exorcisms, and seventy-two of them attested to having been able to do so (Lk. 10:17). Exorcism is as much a part of the New Testament as any other type of miracle, if not more so.

Being that so many of the world's most prominent faith traditions (particularly Christianity) have attested to the reality that dark and malevolent forces exist in our world, it should come as no surprise that those from the ancient astronaut background tend to agree. The notion that the evil entities around us—and the good entities as well—are actually beings from another planet is widely advanced within this group. Erich Von Däniken stated this belief very clearly, saying:

> "We know from Sumerian cuneiforms that the gods created humans as slaves. Our forefathers could not understand it. They believed, erroneously, that these extraterrestrials are some 'gods.' Because they came down from the sky, they influenced humans, and they had supernatural force. They were not spirits or ghosts. Definitely not."[108]

In other words, the "gods" are actually beings from somewhere else—presumably, another planet—in the cosmos. As he stated, some of these beings had malevolent purposes, like enslaving human beings. Von Däniken's statement that they are not "spirits" or "ghosts" is his way of saying that these are not deities or angels, since that is how many religious believers *errantly* describe these types of beings. I will return to this point in chapter four.

So, which is it: beings from another planet, or beings from another realm? Are the religious traditions that describe evil entities as "demons," "fallen angels," and all other manner of metaphysical description, correct? Or, are the ancient astronaut theorists correct in their belief that the ancient peoples had mistaken the "gods" for interplanetary

---

[107] While the other gospels also record this accusation, John alone mentions it four times (7:20, 8:48, 8:52, and 10:20).
[108] See "Dark Forces" on *Ancient Aliens* (S8E4) for this statement and its context.

visitors? Before answering that question, it is important to make note of the common ground on display here. Both religious believers and ancient astronaut theorists agree that there are actually beings of higher intelligence and power in existence, and that some of these beings are evil and destructive in nature. In some sense, both are right about this phenomenon. Both are honest enough to recognize that we are not alone, and that much of the evil on display throughout history is best explained by beings that are greater than us. But the question is much the same as it has been, and will be, in this book: which type of being *best explains* those forces that are discussed within a text like the Bible, and are experienced in our world?

Whether we are looking at examples of possession from ancient texts or the testimonies of those who have been overtaken and controlled by the forces of evil, there are several important factors to consider. The first factor is the "invisibility problem." Say you have a person who begins to act aggressively towards others, exhibits extraordinary strength, speaks in other languages, displays knowledge of things they could not normally know, acts involuntarily or contrary to his or her typical nature, or any combination of these things: where exactly is the being who is manipulating them? Where is the "controller"? When Jesus cast a "legion" of demons out of an individual (or *individuals,* depending on the account) and into a herd of pigs, no one physically observed the demons as they were propelled between the two parties. No one ever saw the demons in any of Jesus' exorcisms.

If we were dealing with an alien being from another planet, solar system, or what have you, wouldn't we be able to see them as they possessed their victim? An alien is flesh and blood (of *some sort*), right? They should have physical appearances. One might postulate that they are wearing some type of cloaking device. Sure, we can postulate anything. But such a claim must somehow be substantiated, or at least rationalized. We cannot simply make all of this up as we go along. The fact that an alien from another place in the material world should be detectible remains a serious problem.

The second major issue is what I would call the "spatial problem." In order for a material alien from another place within the cosmos to possess someone on Earth, they would need to travel a great distance to do so. Even if they had mastered interdimensional travel, or something of the sort, there would still be a tremendous problem. How exactly does a being from another planet fly across the universe, land on our planet, and possess someone, without leaving the slightest trace of its presence? Ah, I've got it Watson—both the aliens *and* their flying crafts are enhanced by a highly advanced cloaking agent, so neither one is visible to the naked eye! I'm afraid that we cannot have it both ways. One cannot hold that aliens have visited our world via spacecraft, while also holding that they would not be in any way visible or detectible. This is a big problem when we are talking about issues like possession or spontaneous human combustion.

The alternative? You probably already know it; the supernatural, metaphysical beings that are described within the Bible (and many other religious texts) truly are supernatural and metaphysical. Demons really are beings of another form and fashion, and they are not confined within our realm of existence. That is essentially what the term "metaphysical" means—something that is other-than or transcendent-from the physical world we live in and understand. Note that "metaphysical" does not mean "immaterial," and it does not mean "ghost" or "spirit," but I will get to that in the next chapter. The point at the moment is that the beings that are responsible for influencing us without being seen must exist not somewhere in space, but somewhere in another realm or dimension.

These beings can negatively affect and influence us without having to fly across the cosmos or travel on a ship. They can obtain or release control, in an instant, because there is no spatial separation between them and us. As Christians, we *already believe* this to be true. This is evidenced in every example of biblical exorcism previously mentioned, and those unmentioned. In all of these instances, demons had control over a human being and were then cast somewhere else. All the while, no one saw them travel through outer space or step into some spectacular spacecraft to zoom off into the sky. This is precisely what we see in nearly all other cases of possession outside of ancient texts as well. At the end of the day, it just doesn't seem as though a traditional type of E.T. can account for this peculiar phenomenon.

They Might be Giants

For reasons that I cannot explain, there are certain things that never get any attention. It just so happens that one of these ignored issues is the topic of this section. The matter at hand is giant people. I don't mean the existence of really tall individuals who spring up from time to time, like Yao Ming or other athletes. I mean the existence of mass groups of giants: people who consistently surpass the bounds of normal human size. It doesn't usually make the biggest headlines, but we have uncovered many remains of these types of individuals. This one is truly too strange to be fiction.

On February 9, 1890, a *New York Times* article discussed the archaeological uncovering of a mass grave site.[109] According to the article, the site was found near Pleasantville, NJ, and it housed about fifty skeletons. The remains were believed to be of Native American descent, and there was something truly remarkable about them: many of these people were over seven feet tall! That's right—they were more than a foot taller than the average Caucasian male in the current era. In fact, one of them was measured in excess of eight feet in height.[110] Interestingly enough, they were found entombed with mollusk fossils and other oceanic remains. That appears to be a common phenomenon, and it may

---

[109] See Adl-Tabatabai's article, "1890 NY Times Article: Race of Giants Discovered in New York."
[110] Ibid.

hearken back to the historical reality of a Great Flood (discussed in chapter two).

An example that hits much closer to home for me personally—being born in the area—is the discovery of human remains at the Great Serpent Mound, in Adams County, Ohio. The Great Serpent Mound is, of course, modeled after a giant snake. This should come as no surprise, since serpents have a significant role in the traditions of many ancient cultures, with the Bible being a prime example of this (Satan). Attempts to accurately date the formation of the mound have been hotly debated (as such efforts often are), but the mound is known to be at least 900 years old, and is more likely to exceed 2,300 years in age.[111] The astonishing mound can only be properly seen from the sky (imagine that). It runs an incredible 1,348 feet in length (more than four football fields), and the "coils" of the serpent are generally regarded as corresponding with the lunar cycles.

There is something else to note about the Great Serpent Mound: many believe it houses the remains of more giant people. Another *New York Times* article—titled "Giants of Other Days"—documented this phenomenon, and it was written on March, 5, 1894.[112] This is another document that has been largely forgotten by time. The article reports that Warren Cowen, a local farmer, discovered the ancient graves while on a hunting trip:

> "Upon opening one of the graves a skeleton upward of six feet in length was brought to light . . . In another grave was the skeleton of a man equally large. The right leg had been broken during life, and the bones had grown together."[113]

---

[111] "Serpent Mound," Ohio History Connection.
[112] See "Giants of Other Days," for the full story.
[113] Ibid.

While human remains of around six feet in length do not constitute a "giant" person *by our standards*, the other skeleton may well. That skeleton was mentioned as being "equally large," even though the legs appear to have been missing from about the knee down. This has led many to believe that the man was actually significantly taller than six feet. It is hard to say what other remains may exist around the mound that have not been (or can no longer be) recovered.

These are not the only examples in ancient North America to be reported, either. Not by a stretch. Researcher, Fritz Zimmerman, has written a book entitled, *The Encyclopedia of Ancient Giants in America*. In it, he asserts that there have been at least 888 giant people documented in over forty-seven states within North America. Certainly, giants have been found throughout most other parts of the world as well. Giants are alleged to have been uncovered in South America, Greece, Scotland, Israel, China, and many other locations. But perhaps the most intriguing archaeological find having to do with giants was uncovered in France, during the winter of 1890.

This discovery, dubbed the "Giant of Castelnau," was unearthed in the cemetery of Castelnau-le-Lez, by anthropologist Georges Vacher de Lapouge. His findings were actually recorded in the scientific journal *La Nature*,[114] and they were rather remarkable. Based on comparing the recovered humerus, tibia, and femoral mid-shaft with average-sized human bones, de Lapouge concluded two major things: the remains were definitely human, and they probably indicated a person who would have been about 11.5 feet in height. As is so often the case, the whereabouts of these remains are unknown almost 130 years later. We do, however, know some crucial aspects of this case. The first is that de Lapouge, and three well-respected scientists at the University of Montpellier, examined the bones and felt as though they represented an incredibly tall race of people. Further, we know that the story appeared in *La Nature*, *The London Globe*, and *The New*

---

[114] See Vol. 18, 1890. Issue 888.

York Times.¹¹⁵ The findings also appeared in other journals from time to time, and all the reports seem to correlate with de Lapouge's initial findings.¹¹⁶

Further reason to believe that races of giant people have existed can be seen in the collaborating evidence from ancient artwork. To the early civilizations, it seems that humongous beings were just an everyday part of life. As insane as that may sound, it appears to be true. This reality seemed to be especially prevalent in Egypt, where many Pharaohs are believed to have been between seven and eleven feet tall. This can clearly be seen on the Abydos King List—found on a wall at the Temple of Seti I at Abydos, Egypt—and through drawings near Saqqura, one of which *unquestionably* displays a giant being who is attended by much smaller individuals.¹¹⁷

Turning to another culture, one of my personal favorite examples is commonly dated to around 2250 BC, and it is called the Victory Stele of Naram-Sin.¹¹⁸ This piece of ancient Mesopotamian artwork displays the triumph of the Akkadian King, Naram-Sin, over a group called the Lullubi. In it, Naram-Sin stands victoriously over a plethora of soldiers who just happen to be of a *much* smaller size: about half as big, actually. These are just a couple from among the large quantity of available examples out there, most of which can be viewed through an online search.

But wait a minute, all of this has been settled! The giant skeletons that are alleged to have been unearthed throughout the world, as well as the ones in our museums, are either hoaxes or can be explained away as something else. To be sure, there have been people who have faked finding giant remains. No doubt about it. For just one famous example,

---

¹¹⁵ I refer you to Ken Ammi's article, "On the giant of Castelnau," for additional information.
¹¹⁶ Ibid.
¹¹⁷ See "The Giants of Ancient Egypt: Part II," for these images.
¹¹⁸ This can be clearly seen in "Victory Stele of Naram-Sin," on the Louvre's website.

the 2002 photograph—which was later touted with the headlines, "Giant Skeleton Unearthed"—alleging that *The National Geographic Society* had discovered giant remains has been officially denounced.[119] No such thing had actually occurred, as the picture had been digitally altered.

To go further, we know to a certainty that many crop circles, UFO sightings, ancient texts, possession stories, and more of the like, have been hoaxes. No one is denying that there are fraudulent examples of these phenomena, and of just about every possible thing imaginable. But should the fact that *some* people have attempted to fool us mean that *everything* else should be dismissed? Does it really mean that all of these findings and reports are fake? Perhaps the baby can stay, even if we throw some of the bath water out of the tub. In the case of the giants—as in the others—I feel that it would be extremely rash and disingenuous to reject all archaeological finds, ancient accounts, and artwork that clearly shows giant people, just because some of these examples may not pass muster.

While some continue to see these accounts as fictional stories, it is also believed that those giant skeletons we do (to a certainty) possess can be accounted for with no need of extraterrestrial intervention. Naturally, the giant pharaohs of Egypt—like King Sanakht—are thought only to be cases of biological anomaly.[120] Even the discovery of the "oldest complete skeleton" of a giant near Rome has been unequivocally branded as a natural oddity (nothing more).[121] The skeptics, doubters, naysayers, or whatever you wish to call them, have their typical, ready-made solution to this issue, as they do with anything else that may not fit their ideological agendas.

In this case, the answer is simple: gigantism. Gigantism is a disease that causes abnormal growth in children. This is typically known to occur because of an excess in the production of growth hormone in the pituitary

---

[119] See James Owen's article, "Skeleton of Giant Is Internet Hoax."
[120] See Osborne's article, "Ancient Egyptian Pharaoh is World's Oldest Case of Gigantism."
[121] See Dell'Amore's article, "Ancient Roman Giant Found," for more information.

gland.[122] Naturally, this results in children (then, usually in adults) who are abnormally tall and sometimes overly heavy. Among those known to have gigantism (or similar diseases, like acromegaly) are such names as Giant Silva, John Rogan, and André René Roussimoff, who is better known as "André the Giant."

These individuals, and others, can be easily seen all over the internet. As indicated in their photos or videos, they are truly enormous people: giants. But on the "gigantism explains it all" position, there are a couple of pesky little problems to contend with. For starters, gigantism is a rare medical disease: a *very* rare one, in fact. Only about three people out of every million have some form of gigantism, with around 100 total documented examples existing in the United States to date.[123] That's right: 100 total cases, *ever*. Globally, it is believed that only several hundred cases of gigantism have been reported.[124] Clearly, extremely large people exist because of gigantism and other disorders, as well as through their respective genetic lines; some families are taller than others, as you may have noticed. Of course, I know of no families or communities in which there are scores of people above seven or eight feet in height. Do you?

If diseases that cause abnormally tall people are so rare, can they really account for *all* of the giant remains we have uncovered? If we are being honest, the answer is no. If these disorders are so uncommon—which they obviously are—why would we have a solid collection of remains from these types of people? If they represent such a miniscule percentage of people in the ancient world (and our own), it is truly remarkable that we have *any* remains at all. But we have many dozens or even hundreds, depending on which researcher you might ask. You can perhaps see finding giant skeletal remains on occasion, but even that would be improbable. This simply doesn't add up.

---

[122] Healthline, "What Is Gigantism."
[123] See "16 Interesting Gigantism Statistics."
[124] See Mohamadi and Salvatori, "Neuroendocrine Growth Disorders."

Dr. Greg Little, writing in AP Magazine, further displayed the problem with attributing all ancient giants to gigantism, when he discussed the long-debated way the Smithsonian has presented Native American skeletal remains:

> "In sum, there is a genuine mystery here. The height of many of the individuals entombed in ancient American mounds was far taller than the general populace - far beyond what could be explained by simple chance . . . Skeptics have related that the disorder gigantism probably was the cause of many reports, but they actually cite no evidence for this assertion. It is a weak attempt to explain away and dismiss the issue. Gigantism is exceedingly rare, so rare that there is no actual incidence statistic for it. America has less than 100 cases of gigantism recoded in its history. In fact, the overwhelmingly vast majority of tall people today, those reaching or approaching 7 feet, do not have the disorder of gigantism. The actual percentage of modern humans who reach 7 feet in height is 0.000007%. In the ancient world of America's Mound Builders, the percentage of the population that reached 7 feet in height would have been even lower."[125]

Among other things, this means that finding mass grave sites of ancient people—which we have done many times—is even more meaningful because individuals of massive height should have been rarer then. In a lot of cases, a person of even seven feet in height would have been incredible, much less seeing many people of that size. This meshes well with the ancient artwork we have, depicting beings that are far taller than their counterparts.

---

[125] Greg Little, "The truth about giant skeletons in American Indian mounds, and the Smithsonian cover-up."

The skeptical "solution" aside, how can we explain the phenomenon of giant people? How can we account for entire groups of people that were truly massive in size? This is not something that can be dismissed as garbage or fringe conspiracy talk. This is something we have archaeological evidence for. You can visit these remains in museums, and see them on documentaries. Of course, they are all over the works of the ancients too. One of the prevailing beliefs—for those who are honest enough to acknowledge that none of our naturalistic theories can explain this—is that "giants" were the product of a higher power. They came into existence from extraterrestrial visitors (of some form), who somehow impregnated human women. The method of how these alien/human offspring were formed is debated, of course. Were they the product of sexual encounters, or did they come about by some type of biological engineering?

This is one issue that interstellar visitors could potentially explain. It's plausible that beings from another planet crossed space, came to Earth, and caused women to bear hybrid children. Far-fetched, I know. But on its face, there are no logical reasons why that is not at least conceivable. Such an event would only require an entity who has the intellectual understanding of how to artificially inseminate a human being. In case you were not aware, *we* do these types of things all the time. Could an intelligent entity that has been around since long before us cause a pregnancy? Sure. That would probably be child's play. If not through a sexual act, then certainly through biological engineering.

If all of this talk sounds like superstitious delusion, we would do well to remember something: *we already believe this*. What? Come on—the Bible teaches that more advanced beings somehow impregnated human women, and that these unions resulted in races of giant people? Well, yes—yes it does. In fact, and after much research, I have come to believe that this reality is inescapable. Regardless of how one feels about the scientific evidence, the great Smithsonian debate, the ancient artwork, or whatever else, people who take the Bible seriously should have no issue with the prospect of giant people. It is right there in the text, clear as day, *if* we are willing to accept it.

There probably aren't many people in the world who haven't heard the story of David and Goliath. It may be low-hanging fruit, so to speak, but it's a necessary starting point. Here, we have David—the future king of Israel—facing off against Goliath, who was the best warrior the vaunted Philistines had to offer. The underdog David takes a sling, which was a common weapon of the day that actually wielded deadly power, and sends a speeding stone into Goliath's head. Goliath was really strong, but that sort of precision shot would have killed almost anything without an incredibly tough exoskeleton! From there, David decapitates Goliath, the Israelites win the battle, and all is well (for a brief period of time).

The critical point is that Goliath was supposed to be a massive individual. If we take the Bible's measurements—based on the Masoretic Text—word for word, he was "six cubits and a span" (1 Sam. 17:4), or 9 feet 9 inches tall. Last I checked, that would have made Goliath considerably taller than Robert Wadlow—the man commonly known as the tallest person in modern history—who stood at 8 feet 11 inches. Naturally, this would also make Goliath noticeably taller than anyone known to have had gigantism.

It is true that there is some discrepancy over Goliath's height, and that other sources—such as the Dead Sea Scrolls and the renowned ancient historian, Josephus—tell us that Goliath was really about 6 feet 9 inches tall. This is no small discrepancy, to be sure. But we must also balance this with the fact that respected ancient sources like Herodotus (called the "Father of History"), Diodoras Siculus, and Pliny the Elder all referenced individuals who were seven cubits high.[126] That would equate to a person who is roughly 10.5 feet tall (recall the "Giant of Castelnau").

Even if we hold to the much more conservative estimate that Goliath was actually 6 feet 9 inches tall, he would have been nearly seven

---

[126] See the Benson Commentary, 1 Samuel 17:4.

feet in height. As previously discussed, that is a pretty rare size on its own, especially at that time. This point leads to the much more curious reality of the situation: Goliath was not the only giant in the land of Canaan. Far from it. Before the Israelites dared to lay siege to the land of Canaan, they sent twelve spies to observe its inhabitants. When they returned, their prognosis made most of the Israelites want to run back (once again) into the slave-driving arms of Pharaoh! The report from ten of the spies was short and ominous: "There also we saw the Nephilim (the sons of Anak are part of the Nephilim); and we became like grasshoppers in our own sight, and so we were in their sight" (Num. 13.33).

While the terrified spies were certainly trying to spread a "bad report" (Num. 13:32-35), this tells us something very intriguing: Goliath was not the anomaly. He was not a three-in-one-million example of gigantism. Rather, *he was one giant person among many others*. The Philistines had tribes of huge people. The Jewish spies said it clearly: they were like insects compared to them. There is clearly some hyperbole involved there, but the overall sentiments were obvious. Maybe the miracle is not so much the stone that slew the giant, but the fact that the other giants threw in the towel afterwards.

On that note, we have to go even further back. Who were these Nephilim that the book of Numbers referenced? When did they enter the biblical scene? The word we transliterate as "Nephilim" is actually only seen in the Bible on three occasions, and within only two different events. We see this in the aforementioned account from the spies (Num. 13:33, used twice), but we also see it occur just prior to the Great Flood (Gen. 6:4). That verse reads as follows:

> "The Nephilim were on the earth in those days, and also afterward, when the sons of God came in to the daughters of men, and they bore children to them. Those were the mighty men who were of old, men of renown."

There are no shortage of hypotheses about who the "sons of God" were. Two of the better-known views propose that these were actually mighty kings who took for themselves a harem of women, or that they might simply be human men from the line of Seth (the "Sethite View").[127]

I will not spend extensive time refuting these two theories, because neither—or any view that excludes angelic beings—make good sense of the situation. For starters, it is particularly telling that the phrase "sons of God" (bə·nê hā·'ĕ·lō·hîm) is exclusively used to discuss the angels. This is true in *all* ancient Semitic writings, not just Hebrew. This comes up clearly in Job 1:6, where Satan—who is unquestionably an angelic being—presents himself to God, along with other angels. They too were referred to as "sons of God." This exact terminology also appears in Job 2:1 and 38:7, and Psalms 89:6 is almost assuredly a reference to the same beings (the angels).

This means that if Genesis 6:4 is talking about some normal tribe of human beings, it would be the only known time that humans were called "sons of God" in all of the ancient Semitic writings, the Old Testament certainly included. While that is probably enough to prove that the Nephilim were actually the product of heavenly beings procreating (somehow) with human women—and not some line of normal people—there are other reasons to believe this.

It is clear from the Genesis account that God had a serious problem with these Nephilim entities. The text records that God reduced the age of human beings to "a hundred and twenty years" (6:3), but only after those pesky "sons of God" decided to impregnate women, further corrupt the human race, and produce the Nephilim. It is curious that human beings do seem to be almost capped at living to that age, is it not? Though the text does not state it, it can be easily inferred that these unions between women and the "sons of God" were not mutual in nature. Directly after this, God delivers another punishment to people: He

---

[127] For more information on these views, and others, see Hodge's article "Who Were the Nephilim?"

decides to eradicate everyone on Earth, save for the righteous Noah and his immediate family.

However you look at it, the text is clear that the Nephilim were extremely frowned upon, and God appears to have delivered these drastic punishments—at least in part—because of their activity. He wanted to eliminate them, and the stain they had left in the world. While it is not generally accepted as being part of the Hebrew Bible, the apocryphal Book of Enoch adds its own details to this. Speaking of the time prior to the Flood, it says: "And when men could no longer sustain them, the Giants turned against them and devoured mankind" (7:3). The "sons of God" are also what Enoch refers to as "the Watchers:" those heavenly beings who survey the world, watching over humanity. This theme also shows up in Job 1:6, and the Book of Daniel (4:13, 17, and 23). The issue of the Nephilim and their angelic/demonic progenitors is clearly something that the Bible alludes to, so the Book of Enoch appears to align with accepted biblical teachings on this matter.

Interestingly enough, the Nephilim find their way back into the world again after the Flood. While we are not sure how they re-entered the scene, we do know that God's response to their existence was still the same: destroy them! Of all the groups the Israelites battled in their history, there are a few that have particular bearing on this issue: the Canaanites, Ammonites, and Rephaites (or Rephaim). All three of these groups are associated with giants, or the descendants of the Nephilim.

The Anakites (or Anakim) were also associated with the Rephaites, and are the tribe specifically mentioned as being part of the Nephilim in Numbers 13:33. We even have King Og of Bashan being referenced, specifically because his bedstead was alleged to have been about 13.5 feet in length and 6 feet wide, and was probably fashioned to accommodate his massive body (Dt. 3:11). In the same verse, he was also said to be the only one "left of the remnant of the Rephaim." King Og was from a line of giant people, and he had a giant bedstead. It all adds up.

The common threads between these groups are striking: all were associated with abnormally large people, all were connected to the Nephilim, and most (if not all) were required to be completely eradicated. God specifically asked the Israelites to wipe these types of people off of the map. Prior to Israel's siege on the land of Canaan, God gave them these instructions: "Only in the cities of these peoples that the Lord your God is giving you as an inheritance, you shall not leave alive anything that breathes. But you shall utterly destroy them . . ." (Dt. 20:16-17). The Israelites were instructed to offer terms of peace to the other groups they encountered, sparing (to take as booty) the women, children, and animals, even if they refused the peace offering (Dt. 20:10-15). But what about all of those who were associated with the Nephilim? No such luck; all were condemned to death. Is that really a coincidence? I think not.

There you have it. The most read, copied, researched, discussed, and pondered book in human history is unequivocal on this issue: races of giant people existed. The Scriptures discuss them repeatedly, God flooded the Earth in part because of their conduct, and God's people even battled them throughout Old Testament history. Put that evidence together with the discovery of skeletal remains, as well as the plethora of ancient artwork and traditions that clearly speak to the existence of giant beings, and I would say there is more than sufficient reason to believe that giants were real. At the very least, the concept is not insane or laughable. It would be insane and laughable to simply chalk it all up to kooky superstition. But believe it or not, there are plenty more reasons to believe in the existence of otherworldly visitors. In the next chapter, we will move on to even better evidence, and to the deeper connection that exists between the heavenly beings of the Bible and the aliens proposed by other perspectives.

Chapter Four
The Angel-Alien Connection

In case you have not picked up on it yet, I have some pretty firm beliefs about aliens, extraterrestrials, or any other term that describes intelligent entities beyond our planet. I absolutely believe they exist and, as the title of this book suggests, I believe that God made them. Of course, that may be slightly misleading. I don't think of "aliens" in the exact same way that some do. On the most literal of levels, an alien is simply an entity that is foreign to this world. However, many people—like the ancient astronaut theorists—view aliens as beings that both live on some other planet within our universe and communicate through interstellar travel. I agree with the literal definition; aliens are not from planet Earth. I disagree on the second part: that aliens live somewhere else within the universe, and need to travel across space to get here. To go a giant step further, I actually believe that aliens are angelic beings. Angels are aliens, and aliens are angels.

In parts of the last chapter, I certainly hinted at this reality. There are far too many issues at play to believe that our strange visitors reside on an unknown planet somewhere. How can we attribute phenomena like spontaneous human combustion (SHC), possession events, and the fact that our universe is more or less programmed in mathematical code, to what amounts to an older and more technologically advanced version of us? There are those annoying little problems to deal with, like the fact that beings from another planet should be seen during events like possession and SHC, and the mathematical issue requires nothing other than God-like power. With this being said, there are surprising associations that exist between the typical understanding of aliens and the heavenly beings described within texts like the Bible. In fact, there is a profound connection between them. In this chapter of the book, I am going to focus on how these points of overlap can further help us to make sense of extraterrestrial contact. It may also help people of faith to make sense of their own beliefs.

A *Crick* Word about the Origin of Life

While Charles Darwin's theory of evolution has been the dominant explanation for how life diversified on planet Earth since the latter part of the 19th century—and has been undeservingly dominant, in my opinion[128]—the issue of abiogenesis (how life ever arose in the first place) has never had anything close to a concrete explanation. That may be an understatement; scientists don't have a clue how inorganic (non-living) materials could have given rise to organic (living) creatures. It is just as physicist Paul Davies so candidly said: "Many investigators feel uneasy stating in public that the origin of life is a mystery, even though behind closed doors they admit they are baffled."[129]

Don't allow the academic elite to tell you otherwise. They have opinions, yes, but no materialistic explanation has emerged from the pack as a suitable match for the problem. And what precisely is the problem? Besides the utter impossibility of getting living matter from non-living matter, one of the major issues is the sheer complexity of life. We see this wherever we look, particularly when we examine ourselves. For example, researchers Ron Milo, Shai Fuchs, and Ron Sender—of the Weizmann Institute of Science—have proposed that the typical male body is made up of more than thirty *trillion* cells.[130] Many scientists have actually hypothesized that there could be trillions more than that.

---

[128] Partiality aside, I highly recommend Wayne Rossiter's book, *Shadow of Oz: Theistic Evolution and the Absent God*. In particular, chapter four is helpful in this matter. It powerfully displays the flaws in Darwin's theory, and also shows the utter incompatibility of Darwinian Theory and Christian belief.
[129] Paul Davies, *The Fifth Miracle*, 17-18.
[130] See the study, "Revised Estimates for the Number of Human and Bacteria Cells in the Body," for more details on this issue.

It is not simply the number that is astounding, but the complexity found within each one of those thirty trillion cells. With our ever-increasing understanding of the nature of the cell, we see that even the simplest units of life are anything but simple. When asked on Ben Stein's documentary, *Expelled,* what he would compare a human cell with—in comparison to the extremely basic way that Charles Darwin (and his contemporaries) understood the cell—esteemed philosopher, David Berlinski, simply replied, "a galaxy." Each of those thirty trillion cells is as complex as a galaxy.

Various others have suggested that an individual cell contains more information than all of the engineering on display within entire cities, combined. Harold P. Klein, the "father of Exobiology"—a branch of science concerned with the search for life outside of planet Earth—summarized the complexity involved in even basic life perfectly: "The simplest bacterium is so damn complicated . . . that it is almost impossible to imagine how it happened."[131] Any quick search reveals the myriad of others who have echoed those sentiments. Yes, life is that complicated. It is that complex.

If the cell is such an amazingly intricate masterpiece, it should go without saying that everything comprised of mass collections of cells is all the more astonishing and difficult to explain. The nature of DNA has been another area where we are continuously perplexed. When speaking of Francis Crick's (who is discussed momentarily) "Sequence Hypothesis," philosopher of science, Stephen Meyer, observed the following:

> ". . . it was the idea that along the spine of the DNA molecule there were four chemicals that functioned just like alphabetic characters in a written language or digital characters in a machine code. The DNA molecule is literally encoding information into alphabetic or digital form. And that's a hugely significant discovery, because what we know from experience is that

---

[131] See John Horgan's, "In the Beginning" in *Scientific American.*

information always comes from an intelligence, whether we're talking about hieroglyphic inscription or a paragraph in a book or a headline in a newspaper. If we trace information back to its source, we always come to a mind, not a material process. So the discovery that DNA codes information in a digital form points decisively back to a prior intelligence."[132]

Meyer was right when he wrote this: maybe more than anyone could have known at the time. One might expect to hear such talk from someone like Stephen Meyer—who is the chief proponent of the Intelligent Design movement—but the fact is that other fields of scientific inquiry have lead us to precisely the same realizations about the information contained within DNA.

Bioengineer, George Church, and geneticist, Sri Kosuri, were able to store roughly 700 terabytes—that is, 700,000,000,000,000 bytes of data—in a single gram of DNA.[133] The experiment was performed at Harvard's Wyss Institute. This speaks to the incredible complexity and storage capacity within the basic building blocks of our genetic structure. More than that, new studies are suggesting that certain genes—even so-called "pseudogenes," which have typically been alleged to be useless leftovers of evolutionary history—code for RNA *both* forward and backwards.[134]

In other words, the code functions in opposite directions, reading left and right simultaneously. That type of complexity is just absurd: far too intricate to have arisen without a "programmer," so to speak. This reality is not lost on those who are experts in computer code, either. When considering the topic of biological information, Bill

---

[132] "Can DNA Prove the Existence of an Intelligent Designer?" Biola Magazine.
[133] See Sebastian's article, "Harvard cracks DNA storage, crams 700 terabytes of data into a single gram."
[134] RNA, like DNA, is one of the major macromolecules essential in all forms of life. Also see Tomkins' article, "Bewildering Pseudogene Functions Both Forwards and Backwards," for more about this incredible phenomenon.

Gates once made the following remark: "Human DNA is like a computer program but far, far more advanced than any software ever created."[135] Clearly, Gates would know about such things. The reality that DNA contains a type of highly advanced informational code, and that the best explanation for this informational code is that it has been written by some type of intelligent being/s, is a reality that crosses many realms of science. It now seems to be an inescapable conclusion; if we are willing to be honest, of course.

The more we understand about the nature of the cell and human DNA, the less "natural" it all looks. Science has not explained how life originated on Earth, and it may not even be *capable* of accounting for the incredible complexity of life with any naturalistic hypothesis. By "naturalistic," I mean undirected and not guided by an intelligent cause: arising naturally, without intervention. At some point, these types of explanations—which simply do not allow for the possible existence of something like an intelligent mind—had to give way to less conventional ones.

Enter the theories of panspermia. Broadly speaking, the term "panspermia" refers to the idea that the basic compounds responsible for life originated elsewhere in the universe, then somehow ended up on Earth, and developed from there. Life began somewhere else, and found its way here. Nobel Prize-winning molecular biologist, Francis Crick (with chemist Leslie Orgel), hypothesized that the difficulties in explaining both the origin of life and its incredible complexity may be best explained by intelligent beings from somewhere else in the cosmos. In simpler terms, extraterrestrials are responsible for life on Earth. This view was called "Directed Panspermia," signifying that intelligent beings had "directed" this process on our planet. Yes, a Nobel Prize-winning scientist theorized that aliens seeded life on Earth.

One of the primary reasons for Crick's hypothesis was the aforementioned complexity of DNA. Having co-discovered the nature of

---

[135] Bill Gates, *The Road Ahead*, 228.

the DNA molecule with Dr. James Watson, Crick knew as well as anyone what type of incredible engineering was involved within it. Specifically, the DNA molecule overwhelmingly appears to have been intelligently engineered. Bear in mind that Crick was not some Jesuit priest or worldwide Christian evangelist; he was a man cut entirely from the cloth of secular science. I suspect this is the only reason why his suggestion that a higher intelligence was responsible for the creation of life was permitted to begin with, much less why it is still around today. If he had been a professed theist, I doubt that Directed Panspermia would ever have seen the light of day.

But that's just it—the *scientific* theory that life on Earth actually began somewhere else in the cosmos is not only still around, but is more prevalent than ever. This is one of the dirty little secrets that the evolutionary community simply does not want the world to know. A 2004 article written by M.J. Burchell in the *International Journal of Astrobiology* discussed, among other things, the mathematical probabilities that life could have arrived here from other places (like Mars) in the universe.[136] A 2012 article in the *Journal of Cosmology*—titled "Transfer of Life-Bearing Meteorites from Earth to Other Planets"—discusses the various issues surrounding panspermia as well.[137] In fact, the entire May 2010 edition of the *Journal of Cosmology* was comprised of articles dealing with the topic, "Panspermia: Transfer of Life Between Stars, Galaxies & Planets." Books have been written as well: Chandra Wickramasinghe's 2014 work, *The Search for Our Cosmic Ancestry*, being one of the more recent examples.

I could go on, but the point should be clear. The notion that life arrived on Earth from somewhere else—and quite possibly by design—in the universe is not a fringe idea, but has been advanced by highly trained, intelligent scientists from around the globe. Frankly, the notions that "God is not a scientific hypothesis" or that we do not possess any

---

[136] M.J. Burchell, "Panspermia today."
[137] See the article, "Transfer of Life-Bearing Meteorites from Earth to Other Planets" in the Journal of Cosmology.

scientific evidence for beings of higher intelligence is outlandish. It takes a lot more faith to believe that all of the aforementioned realities can be explained away as chance or happenstance than it does to accept that at least *some* of them cannot be. As I said earlier, if *any* of this proves the existence of beings other than ourselves, then there actually are beings other than ourselves. With that said, we are back to our central issue. Did extraterrestrials from another planet seed life on Earth and engineer our progress, as ancient astronaut theorists suggest? Or, is a metaphysical being like Yahweh responsible for the creation and proliferation of the human race, as billions of Jews and Christians profess?

Concerning the issues of abiogenesis and the complexity of life, there is one tantalizing little detail that may help us decide which type of beings we are talking about. In scenario one—the ancient astronaut scenario—extraterrestrials arose somewhere else within the universe, propagated their own race, and became advanced enough to create ours. Personally, I don't find this to be insane or irrational. Look at what we have done here on Earth. We have gone from living in huts, scribbling on stone tablets, and riding only on the backs of beasts, to building mansions, publishing electronic tomes, and sitting behind airliners with autopilot capabilities. Why couldn't a group of beings do that somewhere else in the cosmos? It's plausible, let's face it. Given more time, they could potentially have done much more than that. Given enough time, *we* will do more than that.

But there is always a catch. In this case, there is a very big catch. Let's say all of that is true, and a group of beings civilized their own planet, and then began that process here. We still have a major problem: how did *they* come to exist? Remember, we just saw that we are nowhere near being able to explain how life could have come into existence from non-life: how life originated to begin with. In fact, abiogenesis is so problematic that highly skilled (and highly admired) scientists have proposed that life could only have originated on this planet if other beings planted it here. You know what this means. It means we must apply that same reasoning to the beings who may have put life on Earth. If it required an intelligent entity (or entities) to initiate life here, then it required an intelligent entity to initiate life there. They needed a "creator" too. More than that, so did the being/s that made them, and the being/s that made the being/s that made them, and so forth.

But we realize this type of explanation cannot work. It cannot work, in principle. This could certainly tell us how life began here, but it could not give us a full account of how life exists in general. This endless cycle is what philosophers refer to as an "infinite regress" of events, and it is a logical fallacy. In this case, you cannot have an endless line of intelligent causes that are required to give rise to new ones. At some point, there had to be a *first* being. This means that the first being would have no cause for its existence. Essentially, that first being presents the same problem that we see with explaining the origin of life on our planet. We have not solved the problem; not in any way. Rather, Directed Panspermia only pushes the problem back infinitely into the past, and it still holds that intelligent entities are behind it all.

Great, we don't have to explain the cause of our existence anymore! But wait, now we have to explain the existence of those who set the whole thing in motion. For this reason—and the others that have been mentioned—ancient astronaut theory cannot really account for life on planet Earth. Well, better said, it leaves us with a gaping hole. The rise of another race of beings elsewhere in the universe could never be properly accounted for. Their existence cannot be explained any more than our own.

The alternative is something more like the biblical understanding of God. In any form of traditional Jewish, Christian, or Muslim views of God, it is believed that the great Creator is uncaused. God never "came into existence." On these views, God always existed, and always will. Believe me, I take issue with many "traditional" views within my own (Christian) faith. *The Death Myth* is absolute proof of that fact, where I challenge the ideas that people die and go straight to heaven or hell, that the heavenly beings are unembodied, that ghosts or spirits roam the world, and a slew of other beliefs. But here, we find a place where the traditional view seems to best account for the evidence in hand. The only way out of the infinite regress of creators is to believe in a Creator that did not require another for its existence. Not that this is a simple pill to swallow, either, but it seems to be a necessity.

Now, let me be clear about something. If the discussion were simply about whether *any type* of intelligent being created life on Earth, or life was simply the product of unguided, natural causes—in other words, atheism versus deism—things would be a bit different. In that case, we would not need an explanation for the explanation, so to speak. Saying that a god of some sort is the best explanation for life on our planet would *not* require us to explain that god's existence; "who made god?" would not be a question we would need to answer, because it would be a secondary issue at that point. I have written extensively about this elsewhere.[138] However, when discussing whether someone like the God of the Bible or the aliens of ancient astronaut theory are responsible, the question of where these entities come from is valid. We would be distinguishing between two intelligent causes for existence—two competing ideas of the same type—and not between an intelligent cause and an unintelligent cause.

If we do not choose to believe in an uncreated Creator, we are forced to accept something that we know is essentially unexplainable here on Earth—that life can simply spring up from non-life. Even if life arrived on the back of a meteorite, or was seeded here by another life form, *that* life (or some life before it) must itself have come into being from non-life. Inorganic materials must have given rise to organic ones at some point in time. Through the lens of the general scientific community, the only way out of this mess is either to hope on the unknown, or to wish on the future. Scientists from many fields are experts at both practices.

---

[138] See *Mind Over Matter: The Necessity of Metaphysics in a Material World*, 52-55.

We could say, "Well, for all we know, it might be completely possible that life simply emerged somewhere else." Nowhere has this naturalistic dream been more voiced than with regards to abiogenesis. The Nobel Prize winner, George Wald, provided us with a perfect example of this thinking when writing in *Scientific American*:

> "However improbable we regard this event, or any of the steps it involves, given enough time, it will almost certainly happen at least once. And for life as we know it, once may be enough. Time is the hero of the plot . . . Given so much time, the 'impossible' becomes possible, the possible becomes probable, and the probable becomes virtually certain. One has only to wait; time itself performs miracles."[139]

I find this to be especially ironic, considering how many times I have been told that "science requires no miracles." It's funny how miracles are perfectly acceptable, so long as God is not the one doing them.

We could also say, "Well, someday we will have a scientific understanding of how abiogenesis happened." But this is what we could call "science of the gaps;" we have inserted some unknown scientific explanation in as a placeholder, until a real one emerges (in theory). The alternate charge is often used against those who believe in a god or an "intelligent designer" of any sort. It is said that people from these stripes have to put god in as a placeholder, in order to explain things that science has not yet explained, but "certainly will." This objection does not work, particularly with regards to the issue of abiogenesis. God is actually an inference based on real evidence about what was/is necessary for the existence of life, not on things we are yet to uncover.

As far we know *right now*, an uncreated Creator is the best explanation for, among other things, how life could ever have begun on Earth (or anywhere). When we factor in the aforementioned complexity

---

[139] See the article, "The Origin of Life," for this statement and others from Wald.

of life issue, God becomes all the more likely. To wrap up this section, the evidence suggests that we need two things. First, we need an intelligent source that created life on our planet. Second, we need an ultimate source that itself is not reliant upon another for its existence. An alien from another planet could hypothetically satisfy the first criterion, but it cannot satisfy the second.

Physical Beings

Perhaps the greatest point of overlap between ancient astronaut theory and religious views of God and the angels can be found in the outward appearance of these entities. With regards to this subject, ancient astronaut theorists seem to better understand the biblical view of the heavenly beings than most believers do. It somewhat pains me to say that, but I truly believe this to be the case. In ancient astronaut theory (AAT, from here on), extraterrestrial beings are believed to have visited our Earth in ancient times, where they spurred on technological innovation and aided us in our overall cultural development. That is not to say that these extraterrestrials ceased communication with us afterwards, but simply that they at least communicated with us early in our history. As I have pointed out, I believe the notion that the ancient civilizations were helped by more intelligent beings is about beyond dispute; the overall evidence is very strong.

  Another place where AAT is completely on target is that they view the extraterrestrials as physical entities. They have bodies, occupy spatial location (they exist somewhere and not in all places), and are not entirely different than us. Aliens are believed to appear in the flesh (of their own variety), journey around in their advanced aircrafts (of their own type), and physically travel within the universe. As Von Däniken said, these are not "spirits" or "ghosts."[140] As I mentioned earlier, Giorgio

---

[140] See "Dark Forces" on *Ancient Aliens* (S8E4).

Tsoukalos—an extremely well-known proponent of AAT, and also known as "the guy with the crazy hair"—makes this view extremely clear:

> ". . . in my opinion, angels do not exist. Angels were merely a misinterpretation of flesh and blood extraterrestrials, who descended from the sky with means of technology. And that is what these (quote, unquote) 'angels' used."[141]

In AAT, aliens are sort of a "ratcheted up" form of us. But the suggestion that angels are, in some respects, more advanced versions of human beings would cause great distress for many religious believers. I have seen this firsthand. This is especially true if we were to draw any physical parallels. It has almost become an unquestioned (and unfounded) assumption within the church that both God and the angels are immaterial beings. They do not have bodies of any type.

This is yet another case where we are rejecting something that we should *already believe*. The book of Hebrews points this out quite clearly:

> "What are human beings that you are mindful of them, or mortals, that you care for them? You have made them for a little while lower than the angels; you have crowned them with glory and honor, subjecting all things under their feet" (2:6-8, NIV).

I particularly enjoy the way the NIV translates this particular passage, where it says, "You have made them *for a little while* lower than the angels" (emphasis, mine). This speaks directly to the biblical teaching that we will one day be like the angels. Not only that, we will *physically* resemble them. We will have the same type of bodies they have. To prove this belief, we briefly turn to the one human being in history who has already received this new body.

---

[141] See "Aliens and Sacred Places" on *Ancient Aliens* (S3E3).

In the New Testament, there is a profound connection between the death of Jesus and his subsequent resurrection. While his death (the Crucifixion) is believed to have brought about the atonement for humanity's sins, this incredible event would mean nothing if Jesus had remained dead. Paul made this clear when he said, ". . . if Christ has not been raised, your faith is worthless; you are still in your sins" (1 Cor. 15:17). It's a straightforward point: if there was no Resurrection, there was also no Atonement, and certainly no salvation. Despite all of the miracles, Jesus would just have been another dead man. But the Bible holds that Jesus was raised from the dead, and that he came back with a body that was different than the one he previously existed with.

After Jesus returned from the grave, it was apparently very hard to recognize him. Just about every person he previously knew was unable to do so. Mary Magdalene mistook him for the local grave gardener (Jn. 20:15), which I take to mean that she had no idea who the man was, but was sure who he was *not*—Jesus. After the Resurrection, Jesus' disciples saw him calling to them from the seashore, but they only realized it was him after they hauled up a miraculous catch of fish (Jn. 21:4-7).

In the most telling event of all, two of Jesus' former disciples walked (and talked) with him all the way from Jerusalem to Emmaus. At no point during the seven-mile walk did the two gentlemen pick up on the fact that it was Jesus standing next to them (Lk. 24:13). They only realized it was him after he blessed their meal in his familiar style (Lk. 24:30-31). Wouldn't you be able to recognize a friend if you had spent that kind of time with him or her? I have chronicled many more examples elsewhere,[142] but the previous events should prove that Jesus had a new physical appearance: a new body.

So, Jesus rose from the dead with a new body. But what type of body did he have? We already saw that the new body did not physically look just like the old one; the man Jesus did not look identical to the risen

---

[142] See *The Death Myth*, pages 132-133 in particular, for more about this issue.

Jesus. Strangely, Jesus—with his resurrection body—was also capable of disappearing and reappearing at will. On one occasion, Jesus just up and vanished from his disciples' sight (Lk. 24:31). On another—on *two* occasions, actually—he either passed right through a locked door, or sort of "transported" himself from outside the room to within it.

> "On the evening of that first day of the week, when the disciples were together, with the doors locked for fear of the Jewish leaders, Jesus came and stood among them. . . A week later his disciples were in the house again, and Thomas was with them. Though the doors were locked, Jesus came and stood among them" (Jn. 20:19, 26 NIV).

Jesus had appeared from nowhere, even though a locked door should have prevented him from doing so. The allusion here is clearly that Jesus appeared in a supernatural way, not that he simply picked the lock or broke down the door.

From a biblical perspective, it would be nearly impossible to deny that Jesus has a resurrection body. We can also reason that the angels have similar types of bodies; they are not "ghosts" or immaterial "spirits." Jesus pointed out that risen believers will be "like the angels in heaven" (Mt. 22:30). The apostle Paul told us that angels have the same type of perfected bodies that believers will eventually possess:

> "The first man (Adam) is from the earth, earthy; the second man (Jesus) is from heaven. As is the earthy (Adam), so also are those who are earthy (us); and as is the heavenly (Jesus), so also are those who are heavenly (angels). Just as we have borne the image of the earthy (Adam), we will also bear the image of the heavenly (Jesus)."[143]

---

[143] 1 Corinthians 15:47-49. Please note that I have inserted the words within the parentheses to clarify for the reader exactly what was intended.

This was Paul's sophisticated way of saying something very practical: while human beings currently have the type of body that the fallen man (Adam) had, we will eventually have the type of body that the perfect man (Jesus) has. The angels already have "spiritual bodies," as Paul often called them.

Other pieces of evidence could be mentioned, but there is not a *single* example of an unembodied angel appearing in the entire Bible. Not one. The view that angels are immaterial beings has virtually no footing whatsoever. Yes, angels and demons are sometimes referred to as "spirits," but this tells us more about our incorrect understanding of the term than anything else. Typically, "spirits" are considered to be entities of a higher level or quality; in the Bible, "spirit" seldom equates to "immaterial being." Angelic beings (fallen or not) show up in physical form most of the time, and are simply "unseen" (not "immaterial") the rest of the time. Demonic possession is a perfect example of this fact. Remember, one of my biggest points in this book has been that heavenly beings can simply move into our realm from their own. For this reason, they better explain many of the examples of extraterrestrial contact than something like a being who travels here from another place in the universe.

The church has done a disservice to others (like the aforementioned Erich Von Däniken) by telling them that heavenly beings are unembodied, like ghosts or specters. No wonder the ancient astronaut theorists feel they need to refute certain religious beliefs about greater beings; they are only going on what others have errantly told them! I believe they might feel differently, if they thought these entities were actually physical in nature.

I apologize for the brief Christian theology lesson, but I assure you that it is relevant. You see, AAT holds that the beings who created us and have helped human civilization to flourish are flesh and bone (of some sort) beings. While their bodies are almost assuredly not exactly like ours, they have bodies nonetheless. This is a powerful connection that can be made: a link between AAT and biblical teaching. *We already believe* that the angels are more physically and intellectually advanced versions of us (while they are of course more powerful as well). We also believe that the "extraterrestrials" (the angels) have bodies. At least, *we ought to believe this*. I am well aware that many Christians would disagree here, but they shouldn't. The Bible itself is clear about this point. In just the brief evidence I previously discussed, that should be obvious.

Not only is this a clear parallel between AAT and the Judeo-Christian tradition, it also helps to compound the evidence. The extraterrestrials that have communicated with us are different than us; they possess both physical and intellectual superiority. However, they are also very much like our race. They have bodies, and live in tangible worlds. They also exist in certain locations (unlike how God and the angels are often viewed), and make their way to us. I would argue that the angels live in heaven: an unseen realm that lays over top of our own, like a sheet or a film.[144] Often times, the truth of these matters lies somewhere between the typical Christian view—the one that most of us have been taught—and the ancient astronaut view. These two perspectives often intersect in what I like to call "the biblical view."

In AAT, the general thought is that extraterrestrials live on another planet somewhere within this universe, and that they travel to our world in their advanced spacecraft. I have described why that idea might fail to adequately explain much of the phenomena we have experienced and recorded. That aside, we resemble those who are greater than us. I pointed out that in good Christian thought, we will even possess the same types of bodies that both Jesus and the angels have. But we should give the ancient astronaut theorists credit on this—they openly embrace the physical nature of extraterrestrials. In time, maybe more Christians will be willing to adopt the biblical understanding of things, and do the same.

---

[144] I discuss this in detail in *The Death Myth*. See pages 89-99, entitled "It's All Substantive."

UFAs: Unidentified Flying Angels

At the end of the last section, I mentioned the ancient astronaut view that extraterrestrials utilize sophisticated means of transportation in order to visit humanity. If there is anything I know about how the issue of extraterrestrials is viewed within the church, I know that there are mixed feelings about it. To some, there is incredible intrigue surrounding the topic; there are Christians (like myself) who see this as an issue that might help us to better understand God's creation. To others, there is a tremendous fear connected to the terms "aliens," "extraterrestrials," "UFOs," "spacecraft," "flying saucers," or any of the like.

For some reason, the thought that God may have created other beings can be scary. The thought may be that it would make us less special to God. I mean, could the Son of God have become a member of every intelligent race out there, and died for their sins as well? If we were the pinnacle of God's creation, wouldn't the existence of other beings completely undermine that? As I will discuss a little later on, I don't believe there are other intelligent races *within* the universe. However, I have already pointed out that every Christian should *already believe* that God created other beings. In fact, they should also believe that those beings are a bit ahead of us in the pecking order. But there remains the issue that I opened up the book with—we have documented the existence of unknown crafts that we simply cannot explain.

Anyone who has spent time researching the documentation of UFOs may have noticed one of the most interesting things about them: they do not appear to be hostile. I know of very few examples—at least, among the ones that have legitimate documentation—where UFOs or UAPs (unidentified aerial phenomena) are found to deliberately attack a human being or a human aircraft. We have to wonder why that is. Crafts that are documented as displaying unimaginable flight capabilities, the ability to disarm our equipment, and even evade fire with absolute ease, could surely return fire on us. It is no stretch to say that a flying machine of that sophistication could also wreak havoc on human beings, if they wanted to.

My point in bringing this up is that the pilots of unidentified crafts seem to have a peaceful agenda. In the next section of the book, I discuss places where this may not *always* be the case. But on the whole, it certainly appears that they mean us no harm. I can think of a particular type of entity that would also have no plans of harming us. Watching, observing, perhaps even protecting, yes. But harming? No. I am of course speaking of the angels again. Now, the doomsday prepper among us may object, suggesting that the UFOs are really scouting out the progress of human civilization. But someday, they will return and try to completely overtake us, like the creatures on the movie *Signs*!

It could certainly happen. Again, it's *possible*. But this view is another case of ignoring the evidence we actually have to work with. Further, if that were their intention—to annihilate all of humanity at some point in the future—why wait? Hey, I have an idea: let's wait until those puny earthlings have the most advanced sonar, artillery, and transportation options possible at their disposal, and *then* we'll go take them on. We should also make sure they have thousands of years to document our visitations, and to inform themselves on what amazing vehicles we are sporting. While we're at it, let's wait until they have even less natural resources on their planet for us to take as booty. Yes, that will be the time to strike! A future attack is simply unrealistic.

Clearly, playing the waiting game would do nothing to help a civilization that is set on taking over our planet. Whatever we could potentially have to offer them, biding their time in taking it would be utterly foolish. If they don't want what we have, what is their purpose in monitoring our behavior? None of us know the answer to this question, at least not with any degree of certainty. We can reasonably suggest some possible reasons, however. For starters, maybe their mission is to ensure that the human enterprise is actually prospering. They may have a vested interest in our well-being. More than that—and this is just speculation—

they may actually care for the human race. Again, we don't see them shooting anything at us, even though we have fired at them on many occasions.[145] Another suggestion is that the UFO pilots are providing these spectacles as evidence of their existence. That is, as evidence that there are beings who are responsible for creating us. Both of these things are simply reasonable guesses. If either reason is correct (or if both are), there would clearly be religious connotations associated with UFO sightings.

Where have we heard of beings that visit humanity in order to watch over us, show themselves to us, and, when necessary, even come to our aid? Where have we heard of beings who also possess some type of advanced transportation technology? We have read about this in the Bible, of course. There are not many examples where angels appeared in flying machines, but there are a *sufficient* number of examples.

The most obvious event that comes to mind for most of us is Ezekiel's fantastic experience, which is recorded at the beginning of his prophetic book. I am not going to provide the entire first chapter, because it is rather long,[146] but there are a few really telling items we should pull from it. What follows is a carefully chosen cross section of phrases from Ezekiel 1:

> ". . . the heavens were opened and I saw visions of God. As I looked, behold, a storm wind was coming from the north, a great cloud with fire flashing forth continually and a bright light around it, and in its midst something like glowing metal in the midst of the fire. Within it there were figures resembling four living beings. And this was their appearance:

---

[145] Leslie Kean shows many examples where highly qualified military personnel have not just encountered UFOs, but have actually even attempted to take them down. Amazingly, these crafts do not return fire, and always seem to be about impervious to whatever we have to offer. See Kean's book *UFOs*, 83, 94-96, and 151, for just a few of these examples.

[146] I strongly encourage you to read the entire chapter for yourself.

they had human form . . . and they gleamed like burnished bronze . . . Now as I looked at the living beings, behold, there was one wheel on the earth beside the living beings . . . The appearance of the wheels and their workmanship *was* like sparkling beryl . . . high up, *was* a figure with the appearance of a man. Then I noticed from the appearance of His loins and upward something like glowing metal that looked like fire all around within it."

Clearly, the prospect of spinning wheels, flashing lights, glowing metal, and plenty of fire (exhaust?), all allude to some type of flying craft. Throw the "four living beings" (pilots?) into the mix, and that conclusion seems inescapable.

Amazing as it is, one mysterious account does not necessarily warrant the belief that there are UFOs in the Bible. But it doesn't need to; there are other examples to consider. The prophet Elijah was actually privileged enough to witness one of these heavenly vehicles close up. Just prior to becoming only the second person in biblical history to be taken straight to heaven (Enoch was the first), Elijah was swept away to heaven right in front of Elisha: "As they were going along and talking, behold, *there appeared* a chariot of fire and horses of fire which separated the two of them. And Elijah went up by a whirlwind to heaven" (2 Ki. 2:11). One of my personal favorite events in the entire Bible speaks to this issue as well. Just a little while after Elijah was taken to heaven, his successor, Elisha, runs into a spot of trouble.

Having royally frustrated the King of Aram (one of Israel's enemies), the prophet Elisha and his servant found themselves surrounded by an Aramean army:

"Now when the attendant of the man of God had risen early and gone out, behold, an army with horses and chariots was circling the city. And his servant said to him, 'Alas, my master! What shall we do?' So he answered, 'Do not fear, for those who are with us are more than those who are with them.' Then Elisha prayed and said, 'O Lord, I pray, open his eyes that he may see.' And the Lord opened the servant's eyes and he saw; and behold, the mountain was full of horses and chariots of fire all around Elisha" (2 Ki. 6:15-17).

Now, this passage provides evidence for two very important views. The first is that heaven—where God and the angels live—is another realm that is occurring over top of our own, but we are not typically able to see it; the angels were already present, before the human servant could see them. But for the present concern, this also emphatically shows that the angels have a means of transportation. As the text recounts, the mountain was "full of horses and chariots of fire." Was this the same "twelve legions of angels"[147] that Jesus said could be at his disposal in an instant (Mt. 26:53)? Personally, I think that would make a great deal of sense.

While I am persuaded that the angels do have travelling machines—as seen in the several legitimate examples I just mentioned—I also believe it is foolish to try and force that interpretation onto things that clearly do not suggest as much. One of the most popular instances of this is found in the book of Exodus. It records that, during the Exodus (which was when the Israelites "exited" Egypt), "The Lord was going before them in a pillar of cloud by day to lead them on the way, and in a pillar of fire by night to give them light" (Ex. 13:21).

To those who are really looking for it, the "fire" and the "smoke" can be viewed as coming from the exhaust of a vehicle. For that matter, just about any example where God (or an angel) utilizes fire *can be* viewed that way. Judges 13:20 is one I have often read or heard about, and it says, "For it came about when the flame went up from the altar toward heaven, that the angel of the Lord ascended in the flame of the altar." For certain enthusiasts, anything with fire and smoke can automatically include metal

---

[147] It is well-established that, in Jesus' time, a "legion" of soldiers totaled about 6,000 men. That would equate to about 72,000 angels!

crafts, even though the biblical texts seldom discuss them. As I mentioned moments ago, however, Ezekiel's vision does actually mention "glowing metal." But that was specific, not inferred.

I have even read what I deem to be credible thinkers, who insist that things like Jesus' Ascension (when the risen Jesus departed back to heaven) is an example of extraterrestrial crafts;[148] Jesus apparently flew off in one such vehicle, as evidenced by the "cloud" that covered him (Acts 1:9). This cloud, of course, is also thought to be smoke from the engines. But there are problems with this. If Jesus left in a spacecraft, where was the description of the craft itself, of Jesus "boarding the ship," or any of the like? Let's not get too carried away here. These are exactly the types of wild suggestions that cause others to ignore credible examples, such as Ezekiel's vision, Elijah's ride to heaven, and the beings that Elisha's servant suddenly saw on the mountain. We need to reasonably follow the evidence wherever it leads, while making sure not to press beyond its realistic limitations.

In addition to the reliable evidence previously referenced, I could also mention many examples that are recorded in extra-biblical or non-canonical—meaning, those texts that are not included in the list of books that our church councils ratified as divinely inspired—writings, which allude to things like UFOs. In particular, the Book of Enoch has been celebrated as an ancient text that speaks to the issue of UFOs (among other things). But I have narrowed the search down only to information within the Bible itself: information that both Protestants and Catholics should agree was provided to human authors by God. It is perilous to begin citing every possible book from antiquity, because many have some very fantastic—and even absurd—ideas within them.[149] Utilizing a text

---

[148] In his book *Alien Scriptures*, Michael J. Carter makes this claim. While the book is worth reading, suggestions like this tend to strain credibility.

[149] For example, consider what are called the "gnostic gospels." These were written by what amounts to a fringe group that claimed to be Christian, but held to ideas that were often completely opposite of the other biblical writers. In books like the Gospel of Judas and the Infancy Gospel of Thomas, the biblical narrative is turned on its head. The

that we know is fatally flawed at points is a dangerous, and frankly disingenuous, task to undertake.

I realize that I am once again suggesting something that many religious believers will find to be either scary or downright heretical. As I said earlier, many of us are fearful of even accepting that there are aircrafts that were not forged here on Earth. I have gone a clear step further here, suggesting not only that there really are UFOs, but that they are piloted by angels. The thing I do not understand, however, is why many people of faith are so resistant to this idea. Is this not something *we already believe*?

If we were able to tell Elijah, Elisha, or Ezekiel—who were unarguably, and by any possible standard, three of the most respected people of God in the entire Bible—that angels do not have transportation devices, what do you suppose they would say? I didn't really get carried off to heaven? I didn't really see flashing lights, and fiery wheels? The "chariots" that instantly appeared around me were just an illusion? While I cannot tell you for sure what they *would* say, I can tell you that they *would not* respond in these ways. As far as the Bible is concerned, these events really happened. Take it or leave it.

Speaking of those angelic chariots that appear in the Bible, I would be remiss if I didn't address the oddity of that particular choice of words. Why say "chariot," and why mention that horses often accompany these vehicles? Let's start with the chariots. Really, it should come as no surprise that the biblical authors chose to talk about chariots, or that they decided to compare them to the crafts that angels were using. Chariots were the gold standard of travel throughout almost all of biblical history. The Egyptians famously used chariots to pursue the Israelites during their escape (the "Exodus"), where they met a watery fate (Ex. 14:26-28). We know that proceeding powers like the Assyrians and the Babylonians used

---

former actually turns Judas into a hero of sorts, who worked with Jesus to ensure the Crucifixion. In the latter, Jesus (as a child) was a maniacal brat who often used his powers for nefarious purposes.

chariots for many reasons, with battle being perhaps the most established reason. In fact, from about 1700 BC to 500 BC, the chariot was unquestionably the supreme military weapon throughout Eurasia and much of the Middle East.[150]

Even the Romans of Jesus' day employed chariots for transportation (among other things), and so would people for many centuries thereafter. The Hebrew words for "chariot" were *rekeb* and *merkabah*, and the two were used over 160 times (collectively) throughout the Old Testament.[151] Clearly, chariots were everywhere in their part of the ancient world, and they were really the known transportation/warfare crafts. In some sense, "chariot" would have been the ancient equivalent of the modern "vehicle." With all of this in mind, what exactly were the biblical authors supposed to say? "Something resembling a more circular B-21 bomber navigated our space-time continuum, flew around us at supersonic speeds, broke the sound barrier, and proceeded to exit our troposphere." Is that what we should have expected?

Of course not. They used terminology they would have been familiar with at their respective times, just like we do. As I said, the word "chariot" was intended to be "a transportation device," or better yet, "a vehicle." This is basically the way we often describe UFO sightings. Reports like "cigar-shaped object," "round saucer," "triangular craft," and many of the like, are commonplace when people testify to seeing a flying vehicle that cannot be explained. Without question, this is a place where language fails to adequately describe what was seen. Certainly, we can understand that this was true for the people of the ancient world as well. Chariots were the best items of comparison available at that time. That is why they used the term.

And what of the horses? This is one place where I could just make it up as I go, and offer some type of absurd explanation. I could talk about how the horses were really the "engines" that were protruding from

---

[150] See Plubins' article, "Chariot," in the Ancient History Encyclopedia.
[151] Strong's Concordance, 4818 and 7393.

the fronts of the crafts, or some such nonsense. Or, I could simply choose to ignore this issue, because it is difficult to answer (which, for others, is usually reason enough to stop). Instead, I will try to make some sense of this situation. Horses are mentioned all throughout the Bible, so they are extremely common to find in its pages. One of the most interesting aspects of how horses are described within the Bible is that they are always discussed in the context of battle. Beyond a possible allusion in Isaiah 28:28, horses are never discussed as a means of ordinary transportation or for the purposes of farming.[152]

As a connection to this point, horses are also typically associated with kings and other individuals of status or power. After defeating Hadadezer, the king of Zobah, David procured the first Israelite cavalry by taking their forces (2 Sam. 8:3-4). King Solomon (David's son) would go on to increase that number during his reign. Obviously, cavalries are associated with just about every foreign king mentioned within the Old Testament, Hadadezer just being one of them. Even the carriers of God's wrath within the book of Revelation—who are often called the "four horsemen of the apocalypse"—rode upon horses (Rev. 6). Above all else, horses appear to have been beasts of war and creatures that were closely associated with power and nobility.

The occasions when angels were seen in "chariots" *with* horses are rare in the Bible. However, this helps to make sense of something like when Elisha and his servant saw that "the mountain was full of horses and chariots of fire" (2 Ki. 6:17), and when both previously appeared to Elijah (2 Ki. 2:11). Here, the angels—being entities of great power and nobility—were accompanied by the very creatures that were strongly associated with power and nobility. It actually should not come as a surprise, and it would have further designated the power of those beings they were seeing.

---

[152] See "Horse" in Smith's Bible Dictionary.

Does this mean that horses (and other animals) actually exist in heaven? Personally, I see no reason why some types of animals might not exist in heaven (like horses), even if these are animals of a different fashion or quality than the ones here on Earth. Here, I do not mean the spirits of deceased pets; I mean created animals in heaven. The good and intended creation in Genesis 1 had animals within it, animals show up (though rarely, I admit) with the angels, and we know that heaven is a realm of civilization. While that civilization is different than our own, it also has similarities. Can I say to a certainty that animals exist in heaven? No. But that would be a reasonable view based on what little we can glean from the Bible. I think this is much easier to swallow than trying to make some highly figurative metaphor out of the horses, or pretending they weren't *really* there. The horses seen in these instances were indeed some type of equine creatures.

In conclusion, the Bible seems to be pretty clear that angels do have flying machines. Their grand vehicles ("chariots") are a regular sight within the Old Testament. Perhaps it is no stretch to suggest that UFOs, UAPs, and all manner of truly unidentified crafts, were not driven by aliens from another part of the universe, but by the aliens that live in a different realm of existence. By this, I mean the angels in heaven. They are "alien" to our world, and they are the ones we are seeing. This would make sense of the phenomenon that UFOs do not typically display aggressive tendencies towards us: neither do the angels. It would also make sense of why no "takeover" has occurred.

Lastly, it would be consistent with the teachings of the most read and established text in human history—the Bible. Maybe an answer to the UFO question has been there all along, right under our very noses. I recall the words of the famous futurist, Arthur C. Clarke, when he considered the source of UFOs: "One theory which can no longer be taken very seriously is that UFOs are interstellar spaceships."[153] I couldn't agree

---

[153] See CE4 Research Group, "Quotes."

more. The UFOs are really UFAs—unidentified flying angels. These crafts (and their pilots) come not from another place within the universe, but from another realm entirely. The question is: if there are good angels flying about, are fallen angels doing the same?

Angelic Abductions

While we are on the subject of flying crafts and people being taken away on them, this feels like an appropriate time to briefly address the issue of alien abductions. For eons, people from around the world have told of their experiences aboard various extraterrestrial spaceships, and of the entities who were responsible for the events. Based on the previous section, people of faith should have no problem accepting that such events could take place. However, it may not be that simple. We can understand Elijah—a great prophet of God—being carried away to heaven by an interdimensional vehicle, but what about your average person? Are people telling the truth about these encounters, or are they all a big hoax? If they are telling the truth, were their abductors creatures of good or evil intent? In order to answer these questions, we must first describe a few of the most prominent abduction stories on record.

One of the most discussed cases of alien abduction is Travis Walton's account, in which he claimed to have been taken from Earth for a total of five days. The event began on November 5, 1975, when Walton was working at the Sitgreaves National Forest in Arizona as a logger. On his way home one evening, Walton and his six co-workers purportedly saw something like a "shiny disc" hovering in the air.[154] They reported that Walton had gone to investigate the craft more closely, but was struck by some type of shockwave that launched him ten to twenty feet away.[155] After his co-workers had left—presuming he had been killed—Walton was allegedly taken captive on the ship, where the beings on board

---

[154] Lee Speigel, "UFO-Alien Abduction Still Haunts Travis Walton."
[155] Ibid.

attempted to control him. After several days of imprisonment, he was finally released from the ship.

Naturally, Walton has received a great deal of pushback for his account, which later became both a book and a movie.[156] Each of us can judge the overall veracity of Walton's tale, but to me, it is difficult to disagree with his take on the whole situation. In response to his countless critics, Walton summed up the issue of extraterrestrials in the following way:

> "The scientific evidence of the likelihood of intelligent life in our vicinity has become so overwhelming that the people who believe that we're alone in the universe — *those* are the kooks."[157]

While I would not firmly claim that his experience was valid, I think we should take this statement seriously. As you may have noticed, I also believe that the "kooks" are those who completely reject the reality that other intelligent beings exist *somewhere* else. Walton and I would probably differ with regards to where these entities live and what their true identities are, but we are in complete agreement that they are real.

Another really prominent case of alien abduction is that of Betty and Barney Hill, a married couple who claimed to have been jointly captured. More than prominent, many consider this to be the prime or "flagship" example of all known abduction stories.[158] These Portsmouth, New Hampshire, natives' experience came while driving home from vacation in September of 1961. It started with both Betty and Barney seeing a strange light in the sky along Route 3. As they pulled over and began a closer investigation with binoculars, they came to believe this light may actually be a flying craft. As they drove, they saw the item at various

---

[156] Walton's 1978 book was titled, *The Walton Experience*, and the 1993 film was titled *Fire in the Sky*.
[157] Ibid.
[158] See Booth's article, "Best Cases of Alien Abduction."

points on their way home. Supposedly, it got weirder when they arrived at the house. They reported that their clothes were inexplicably torn, the car had a strange pattern on it, and that they had somehow lost all track of time.[159] Their conclusion was that they must have been abducted.

There are, of course, many other alleged cases of alien abductions out there. In fact, there are far more than an entire book could properly catalog. Clearly, a great deal of them are not worth considering, based on the completely unrealistic nature of the accounts. Most of us have heard stories about people who said they were abducted by things like "little green men," or even large reptiles![160] There will always be people who really are a bit disconcerted, and at least as many who are simply trying to get attention. While I find a story like that of Travis Walton's to at least be coherent and reasonably described, I have already stated that I am not placing a tremendous amount of emphasis on the issue of abductions. The funny thing is, in its own very strange way, this is also an issue that potentially has some biblical backing. We *may already believe* in abductions!

Let's start with an event that was discussed in the previous section: Elijah's trip to heaven. Recall that the prophet Elijah was taken to heaven in a whirlwind, accompanied by a "chariot of fire" (2 Ki. 2:11). That is, an angelic vehicle appeared in our realm and escorted—or at the very least, helped to escort—Elijah off to be with God. I don't know about you, but that sort of sounds like—and I am just throwing this out there—an *abduction*! Clearly, Elijah was never returned to planet Earth, so this event is not your traditional abduction story. But Elijah seems to have been taken aboard a foreign vehicle that was piloted by an "extraterrestrial" being (an angel), and he was removed from our world. On the whole, the shoe appears to fit. Though we know nothing else about the event, accept that God "took him," a man named Enoch also bypassed death in order

---

[159] See Barclay's article, "The Betty and Barney Hill Abduction" for more information on this account.
[160] See Waterlow's article, "Aliens want to steal my soul" for Samantha McDonald's account of how she has been repeatedly visited by "the reptilians," as an example of this idea.

to live with God (Gen. 5:24). Did a craft take him too? We simply do not know.

While there are no other examples of that exact kind in the Bible, there are a couple that more loosely fit the description of an abduction. The apostle Paul talked about an experience that an undisclosed "man" once had, when he was taken to the "third heaven" or "paradise." This event is recorded in 2 Corinthians 12:2-4:

> "I know a man in Christ who fourteen years ago—whether in the body I do not know, or out of the body I do not know, God knows—such a man was caught up to the third heaven. And I know how such a man—whether in the body or apart from the body I do not know, God knows—was caught up into Paradise and heard inexpressible words, which a man is not permitted to speak."

This is not the place for a detailed study of this passage, but I have done that elsewhere.[161] Most interpreters believe that Paul was actually talking about himself, and the place he went was God's abode itself. Paul was probably the "man" who went to the "third heaven."

Notice that he was not sure whether or not this event happened "in the body"—meaning, he was physically present—or if it had just been something like a vision. That is important to note, because there is a possibility that Paul (or whomever it was) never physically left the world. However, there is also the possibility that he did. It may have been that Paul was tangibly lifted off the ground and somehow taken to the deep recesses of heaven. To talk about the possibility of a flying craft at this event would go entirely too far, as we do not have any indication of such a thing. Still, there is the distinct possibility that Paul had been abducted

---

[161] See "There and Back Again: An Apostle's Tale" in *The Death Myth*, 39-44, for a very detailed discussion of this event.

by God (or an angel), where he saw things that the rest of us simply aren't able to. At the very least, he certainly went there in his mind.

The last example from the Bible that can *reasonably* be connected to the issue of abductions is brought to us by the book of Revelation. In its enigmatic pages, we hear on two separate occasions that its author—which is traditionally believed to be the apostle John, when he was a *very* old man—was "in the Spirit" (Rev. 1:10, 4:2). At these times, John saw many amazing things, like a grand throne that produced "flashes of lightning and sounds and peals of thunder" (4:5). Not coincidentally, he also saw the "four living creatures" that Ezekiel had seen, which was discussed earlier in this chapter. It is difficult to tell if John was seeing the same things that Paul had, but it seems quite plausible.

It is equally difficult to tell if John's experiences were simply visions, or if they were embodied trips to the heavenly realm. Personally, I believe that visions best explain the events. But the fact remains that John (like Paul before him) *may* have been physically taken off of the Earth, somehow, and in some way. This is another possible abduction event.

It was the renowned ufologist, Dr. Jacques Vallee, who famously remarked: "Human beings are under the control of a strange force that bends them in absurd ways, forcing them to play a role in a bizarre game of deception."[162] It has been suggested by some that the UFO phenomenon should be exclusively attributed to fallen angels or their offspring.[163] There is no question that most of the documented UFO cases, along with the biblical information about flying "chariots," points us in the direction of a type of peaceful, or even virtuous, group of intelligent beings. So far as we can tell, the vast majority of UFO experiences do not reflect any nefarious intentions. But where there is good, there is also evil. I personally have little doubt that fallen angels have transportation devices of their own, just like the good angels. Why wouldn't they? Perhaps those abduction events (if true) where people claim to have been terrorized or even harmed are the

---

[162] Jacques Vallee, *Messengers of Deception*, 20.
[163] See Smith's "Nephilim: True Story," at around 58m for an explanation of this view.

products of these demonic entities. All things considered, it seems to be a plausible belief.

It should be clear that, on the whole, I am not putting as much stock in these types of events as I do with some of the others mentioned thus far. Overall, abduction stories are much like near-death experiences in the sense that they are all over the map, and range from the sensible to the completely absurd. We should take them with a large grain of salt. But we would also go too far to say that nothing of the sort has ever, or *could ever have*, occurred. As I mentioned, the Bible actually provides at least some reason to believe in abductions. Admittedly, the events in the Bible—outside of Elijah's assumption into heaven, perhaps—do not perfectly line up with traditional abduction reports. However, we have established that angels actually have flying crafts, and that they are capable of taking human beings away in them. The issue of alien abductions may be sitting on the fringe of believability, but such events are not completely outside the realm of possibility.

Alone in the Universe?

Though my view is that angels—God's first created beings (as far as we know)—are really the ones who have been visiting our planet, there is an extremely important question left on the table: are there any other "aliens" in existence? Are there extraterrestrial entities out there anywhere in the cosmos, living on some distant planet, and have they ever reached out to us? Admittedly, these are difficult questions to answer. I recall reading the late Billy Graham's response when he was asked if the Bible speaks to this particular issue:

> "No, the Bible doesn't say anything about the possibility of life on other planets. Its main concern is with human life on this planet, including our problems and our future. This doesn't mean life can't exist on other planets, for it well might; the Bible simply doesn't tell us."[164]

Pastor Graham was right: the Bible does not tell us about life on other planets. As it turns out, science does not really tell us that life exists on other planets, either.

Naturally, we have no way of knowing with any certainty whether or not there is life on other planets. The universe is simply too vast, and too unexplored, to definitively say one way or the other. But I am completely devoted to the practice of basing our beliefs on the evidence we have in hand. That is my primary problem with most of the modern Christian apologetics strategies. How are we really fostering a solid belief in God, when our reasons for belief are often so abstract and speculative?[165] In this book, I have tried to base my views on things that can be reasonably verified: things we have real, tangible evidence for. At the least, things that we can infer, based on what we do know. But this is precisely why I do not believe there are beings who exist on other planets inside of the universe.

Without question, humanity has made massive strides in our investigation of the surrounding universe. Our epic successes in launching all manner of space shuttles—though we cannot forget our many epic failures to do so—illustrates this point. Satellites have also given us a lot of very interesting information about the Sun, our Earth, a number of other planets within the solar system, and some things beyond it. We have landed robotic spacecraft on the moon, Venus, Mars, a number of asteroids, and the surrounding areas of all the other major planets in our solar system.[166] Since the 1960s, we have also been exploring cosmic phenomena in the gamma-ray, X-ray, ultraviolet, visible, and infrared regions of space. Perhaps most famously, the Hubble Space Telescope was sent out in 1990 to

---

[164] Billy Graham, "Did God Create Aliens?"

[165] Here, I think of things like the *Kalam Cosmological Argument* or universal fine-tuning. "Proofs" like these require a great deal of speculation, and are based on a multitude of assumptions about the way the universe operates. More than that, they are extremely difficult for most people to understand.

[166] "Space Exploration." Encyclopaedia Britannica.

observe the visible and ultraviolet regions of space.[167] Its many amazing images can be seen in both books and images on the internet with ease.

Of course, our exploration of the universe is fantastically incomplete, and it always will be. Consider this fact: we have scarcely even investigated the waters *on our own planet*. More specifically, we have only investigated about 5 percent (or less) of the Earth's oceans.[168] And it's not like we haven't been researching the oceans for a very long time: much longer than we have been traveling through space. So, with all of our achievements, I find the belief that we will ultimately explore most of the universe to be about as realistic as the expectation that we will join forces with "Doc" Brown and invent time travel. I would wager that we will *never* investigate even 5 percent of a vast, and perhaps infinite, universe. For that matter, we don't even know how large the universe is, which makes it impossible to know how much of it we have explored! If there are indeed other entities within our universe, it seems as though they would need to reach out to us. As I have mentioned throughout the book, I think that entities of some sort actually have.

But this has not stopped us from trying to find intelligent life elsewhere, and it shouldn't. Concerning the search for life itself, we have established the SETI Institute—or the Search for Extraterrestrial Intelligence—in order to look for beings elsewhere in the universe. While the general exploration has been going on since the early 1900's, organized, international efforts have really picked up over the last thirty years or so. Officially, the modern SETI era began in 1959, and their underlying mission is clearly displayed on their website:

> "Our current understanding of life's origin on Earth suggests that given a suitable environment and sufficient time, life will develop on other planets. Whether evolution will give rise to intelligent, technological civilizations is open to speculation."[169]

---

[167] Ibid.
[168] "How much of the ocean have we explored?" National Ocean Service.

It's not that I don't find SETI's work valuable, but I have to laugh a little at this assessment. We just saw how extremely difficult it is to explain the genesis of life, but apparently, any "suitable" planet will inevitably beam forth with living creatures. Is that right? I could also dissect the assumption that evolutionary processes can completely explain the diversity of life on Earth, but let's press on.

At one point, SETI had united with NASA on a joint venture, called the NASA SETI program. It was shut down by Congress in 1993, with funding concerns being cited.[170] At that point, Project Phoenix emerged. SETI summarizes the purpose of the project as follows:

> "Project Phoenix was the world's most sensitive and comprehensive search for extraterrestrial intelligence. It was an effort to detect extraterrestrial civilizations by listening for radio signals that were either being deliberately beamed our way, or were inadvertently transmitted from another planet."[171]

The endeavor utilized radio telescopes, which are a type of directional radio antenna that enable the user to detect certain frequencies from space. Since then, they have also employed other efforts, such as Project SERENDIP and another large undertaking in Australia. Much more could be mentioned, but both NASA and SETI have been peering great distances into our surrounding universe and/or listening in for radio contact *at a high level* for at least the last three decades.

During that time, SETI (and NASA, of course) have come away with some really stunning information about space. NASA's website has a very interesting image gallery that allows one to see many of the pictures we have taken of the "Red Planet."[172] All manner of strange and intriguing

---

[169] "SETI Research." The SETI Institute.
[170] Ibid. "Project Phoenix."
[171] Ibid.
[172] See the "images" link on NASA's "Robotic Mars Exploration" tab, to browse all of these pictures for yourself.

pictures are available, and these have most certainly increased our understanding of Mars. We know much more about surrounding planets than we did before such efforts, and we know much more about our own Earth. We cannot diminish the importance of these discoveries. But what about the central purpose of SETI: you know, the discovering extraterrestrial life part? Well, no such luck. None whatsoever. No investigative project has ever definitively found life elsewhere in this universe.

We have heard for decades from astrobiologists, exobiologists, and other space professionals, that Mars, or either Jupiter or Saturn's moons, *may* contain (or have once contained) water, and that they seem to possess the general placement in the solar system to potentially support life. These are just some of our best guesses; the evidence has never panned out. I am sure this is the reason why so many major space projects prove to have short shelf lives, and the funding is often cut rather precipitously.

Now, many of the organizations that have researched UFO and UAP phenomena—not to mention the *vast* array of eyewitness testimonies we possess from the civilian world—have, to me, given us far more than sufficient reason to believe that other beings exist. But remember, the question we have been trying to answer throughout the book concerns the location of these beings; are they from somewhere within the universe, or do they perhaps hail from another realm of existence altogether? The fact that we have absolutely no evidence that a civilization (or even basic life) exists anywhere else in this universe actually helps to answer that question.

Based on everything that has been discussed, the existence of extraterrestrial or alien life—that is, the existence of intelligent beings somewhere besides our planet—seems to be unavoidable. When we compile the religious traditions from antiquity, the astonishing architecture of early cultures, the eyewitness accounts that span millennia, and the investigative reports given to us from organized national projects, it is extremely difficult to ignore that we have been visited by "others." It's just that we

---

https://www.nasa.gov/mission_pages/mars/images/index.html

have no hard and fast reasons to believe these entities came from some other planet, or a distant location within the universe. In fact, that prospect seems wholly inadequate in explaining our extraterrestrial contact.

One final thing should be said in this section. We may well find life on another planet at some point in time. It could happen, and I think there are certainly valuable byproducts of the search, even if we don't find the target of our query. Whether or not those efforts are worth the money we have spent on them is a political debate that I will not take up in this book. In any event, finding *some kind of life* is a far cry from finding life that equals, or even surpasses, our own. Don't get me wrong: any life, anywhere, would be remarkable. This is especially true when we consider the extreme complexity of even the "simplest" organisms (discussed previously), and our complete inability to understand how life could just spring forth from inorganic materials.

If we someday found other habitations within the universe, it would certainly change the way we understand many aspects of life. This would quite possibly help to explain the UFO or UAP sightings that have occurred all over the planet, and for thousands of years now. However, it would not ultimately harm the idea of God, because those entities would still need an intelligent cause for their existence. As I pointed out very clearly in the section "A *Crick* Word about the Origin of Life," there must, at some point, be a being who caused the others; there must be an uncaused intelligence. With that said, the question of whether or not we are "alone in the universe" continues to allude us. At the present, we would have to answer in the affirmative; yes, as far as we know, we are alone. And though we may be alone *in the universe*, we are clearly not alone *in all of existence.*

Chapter Five
God Made the Aliens

Throughout this book, I have discussed some of the supporting evidence for the idea that extraterrestrials exist, as well as who these beings really are. In the final chapter of this book, I want to evaluate what all of this means from a Christian perspective. I am, after all, a Christian researcher. I find everything I have discussed thus far to be incredibly important, but the main purpose of this book is—as the subtitle clearly suggests—to make sense of extraterrestrial contact. Specifically, I want to make sense of it from a viewpoint of faith.

What does this talk about angels, aliens, UFOs, UFAs, incredible ancient architecture, repeating numbers, and all of the like, tell us about the Christian faith? How can it inform and influence our worldviews? Answering these questions is precisely the aim of this final chapter. If you have followed this far, and if you believe that there is some degree of truth in what I have said, then perhaps you are willing to take these matters to their logical conclusions. If you are willing to do that, you may come away with a much bigger picture of both the Christian faith and our place within God's creation.

God of All

Speaking as someone who has been involved within the church for many years, I would like to think that I have a good pulse on how things tend to operate. Musically, I am aware of both our classic hymns and our most contemporary worship songs. I am more than familiar with the divisive, "are you Wesleyan-Arminian, or Calvinist?" sorts of discussions. I understand the quiet tension that still exists between many Catholics and Protestants. I know that preachers with a southern accent magically sound more sincere than those without, and that pastor's wives are supposed be tirelessly supportive, organ-playing wonder women. I know that youth pastors are supposed to wear "skinny jeans" and thick-rimmed glasses, play guitar, and have the basic demeanor of a used car salesman.

Above all else, I know that John 3:16 is probably the most quoted and referenced verse in the New Testament (if not the entire Bible). It would probably be difficult to find a staunch atheist, or even a Third World tribal elder, who hasn't heard this text at some point in time: "For God so loved the world that he gave his one and only Son, that whoever believes in him shall not perish but have eternal life." Yes, this is one of the staples of the biblical message; God loves everyone and everything within the world He has created. Jesus died for *everyone*. We all know it, and we all say it. The problem is that many of us don't believe it. Not really.

Perhaps this point is no more visible than in the way that most of us view other religions. Specifically, this is true of the way we view other ancient accounts. As I showed specifically in chapter two, there are many incredible similarities between the Bible and the ancient texts of other religious faiths. Many scholars and theologians have spent an insurmountable amount of time trying to separate the Judeo-Christian tradition from other religious traditions, and in many respects, rightfully so. There are many issues in which the biblical perspective differs radically, and in theologically significant ways, from other prominent religions and ancient traditions.

Like the Jewish faith that gave rise to it, Christianity affirms the existence of only one God. A monotheistic view of the Divine is, on the whole, different than the polytheism (the belief in many gods) we see in nearly every other ancient religion. That being said, the doctrine of the Trinity or Godhead is not so incredibly different than all polytheistic views in certain respects, particularly the emphasis on *three* entities that seem to be placed and idolized above the rest of the visitors we have had. As I discussed in the section, "Strength in Numbers," this important concept seems to span all of the major (and many minor) religions in the world.

The doctrines of hell, the resurrection from the dead, and the creation of a new heaven and new earth are also often quite different than notions of the afterlife in the other ancient religions. Most specifically, the physical nature of both the resurrection body and the new heaven and new earth differ entirely from Platonic (and other) notions of a purely immaterial afterlife: a view that is extremely prominent in many Greek mythologies and other ancient religions. Above all, there is of course the Christian belief that Jesus was the incarnate (made flesh) Son of God and the Savior of the world. A first century Jewish man was not only the wisest teacher of all time, but literally represented divinity on Earth; Jesus was the one and only "God-man." He represents a dividing line between Christian belief and the beliefs held within *all* other ancient religions (even Judaism). These things certainly distinguish Christianity from other belief systems. These differences are very important, and I am by no means advocating that we should announce full religious pluralism and accept that "all roads lead to Rome," so to speak.

On the other hand, I fear that we have made such an effort to separate ourselves that we have dismissed the incredible similarities we share with many other faith traditions. More than that, perhaps we have missed the fact that these similarities can actually prove valuable in adding credence to our own claims about God and His activity in human history. In the previous chapters, we looked at the impressive similarities between creation accounts and flood narratives. But the connection goes much deeper than that; the Bible clearly teaches that God has great concern for the entire world, and that He always has.

It starts in the beginning, with God creating Adam (meaning literally "man" or "mankind"), not with God creating Jews or Christians. The first ten chapters of Genesis do not deal with any particular group of people, but just simply with *people*. It is not until God calls Abram—later changing his name to "Abraham," meaning "the father of many nations"—that God begins the process of forming a distinct group that He will call His own. But it's not really even until God calls Moses to return to Egypt, in order to reclaim those from the line of Abraham, that a truly distinct assemblage of people began to take shape. That was roughly 430 years after God had begun His salvation plan with Abraham, at least in the apostle Paul's reckoning of time (Gal. 3:17). I, for one, am not going to disagree with him!

A little known (but extremely telling) fact is often ignored concerning the Exodus. Even when the Hebrew people were emerging as God's chosen group, those who were not ethnically Hebrew were also permitted to leave Egypt and join them. Exodus 12:37-38 makes this very clear: "The Israelites journeyed from Rameses to Succoth. There were about six hundred thousand men on foot, besides women and children. Many other people went up with them, as well as large droves of livestock, both flocks and herds." I can only wish this fact were discussed with more regularity.

Other people joined the Israelites? Could these "others" even include Egyptians, the very people who had held God's people captive? Yes, and there is no doubt about it. The astonishing plagues God released on Egypt—and the failure of Pharaoh's magicians to keep pace with them—convinced at least some of the Egyptians to leave their powerful empire and join with the more powerful deity (as they would have seen it), merging themselves with the people of Yahweh.

There are of course many other examples of God reaching out to other nations, even from the Old Testament, where God is often viewed by critics as being some type of evil tyrant. The words of the well-known religious critic, Richard Dawkins, should remind us of such sentiments:

> "The God of the Old Testament is arguably the most unpleasant character in all fiction: jealous and proud of it; a petty, unjust, unforgiving control-freak; a vindictive, bloodthirsty ethnic cleanser; a misogynistic, homophobic, racist, infanticidal,

genocidal, filicidal, pestilential, megalomaniacal, sadomasochistic, capriciously malevolent bully." [173]

Tell us how you really feel, Richard! I would kindly like to suggest that these opinions could not be more groundless. Another very telling example of God's care for the nations—from Dawkins' hated Old Testament—comes to us via a man named Jonah. The book of Jonah records that God sent the prophet Jonah to warn those living in a city called Nineveh to repent of their sins, lest they end up being destroyed. The amazing thing about this—and, as it turns out, the reason why Jonah was so reluctant to complete the mission—is that Nineveh was the capital of ancient Assyria. So, what does that matter?

Not only were Assyrians most definitely not monotheists, much less followers of Yahweh, they were an often-brutal group who were—at that very time—in the process of trying to destroy the northern kingdom of Israel: God's chosen people. While they are said to have actually believed Jonah's message and repented (3:5), their change of heart apparently did not last long. In 722 BC, Assyrian invaders conquered Israel, no doubt killing scores of God's people. Nonetheless, Yahweh reached out to the Assyrians in an effort to save them. I find that to be astonishing. So did Jonah, who—perhaps understandably, given the context of the situation—moped around in disbelief and frustration that God had not eradicated all of them (4:5-11).

The Babylonian empire later emerged as an ancient superpower, and they finished the job that Assyria had started. In 587-86 BC, they conquered the southern kingdom of Judah, pillaged their sacred temple, and took many of the Jewish exiles back to Babylon as slaves. Because of their wickedness towards God's people, Babylon would go on to be a symbol for other evil empires.[174] Shockingly, God commanded His people to try their best to warm up to their Babylonian captors, and pray that

---

[173] This, and other similar statements, was made in Dawkins' *The God Delusion* (pg. 31).
[174] See 1 Peter 5:13 and Revelation 17:5, for example.

things would go well for them (Jer. 29:4-7)! The exile was not simply a punishment for Israel's covenant unfaithfulness; it was also one of God's ways of reaching out to those who were supposedly not a part of the salvation narrative.

The great prophet Isaiah even provided an open invitation to those "foreigners"—which clearly refers to those who were not ethnically Jewish—who were willing to serve Yahweh. Isaiah 56:6-7 records the following: "Also the foreigners who join themselves to the LORD, to minster to Him, and to love the name of the Lord . . . Even those I will bring to My holy mountain and make them joyful in My house of prayer." In the book of Joshua, prior to the conquest of the city of Jericho, a foreign *prostitute* named Rahab aided the Israelite spies who were investigating the city. As a result, God spared her and her entire family. More incredible is the fact that Rahab is listed in the genealogy of the Jewish messiah himself, being mentioned as a person of admirable faith and good works![175] The Old Testament is pretty clear: you *never* had to be born a Jew in order to follow Yahweh and take part in His salvation plan.

It should not come as a surprise to anyone that the New Testament is emphatic about the fact that God is trying to reach out to everyone. Repeatedly, Jesus elevates the Samaritans—a group much-maligned by Jewish people in and around Jerusalem at that time—to tremendous levels. In Jesus' parable of the Good Samaritan, it is a Samaritan man, not the Jewish leaders, who shows compassion to a wounded stranger (Lk. 10:25-37). Jesus even invites a sexually promiscuous Samaritan woman (recall Rahab as well) to change her ways and join the Kingdom of God, the result being that many other Samaritans also came to believe that Jesus was the long-awaited messiah (Jn. 4).

---

[175] See Matthew 1:5, Hebrews 11:31, and James 2:25. Some have speculated that the Rahab mentioned in Matthew 1:5 is not *the* Rahab mentioned in Joshua, but that notion has never truly caught on among biblical scholars. There is no question that she was a person who was both a part of the Jewish narrative and someone of respectability.

Elsewhere, Jesus emphatically claimed that he had come to save lost people (Lk. 19:10), to find the "sheep" who had ventured away from the shepherd (Lk. 15:3-7), and even to restore the children who had both insulted and ventured away from their heavenly Father (Lk. 15:11-32). In fact, the teachings of Jesus and the apostles make it clear that Israel was in fact *never* the endgame at all. Rather, the Jewish people were selected by God for the explicit purpose of reaching out to the rest of the world.

It was through the Jewish people that the most sacred individual in the entire Bible would come forth. I am of course speaking about the messiah, the "anointed one." And what exactly was the messiah supposed to do? Well, that brings us back to John 3:16. As the "conquering King," the messiah was supposed to destroy the forces of evil and establish an everlasting kingdom.[176] That is undoubtedly one facet of the messianic expectation, with Jewish believers often seeing this as one of Jesus' failures, and Christians viewing this more as an example of intentionally unfinished business: something that will happen upon Christ's return.

But the messiah was also supposed to be the suffering servant who would lay down his life for the sins of the world.[177] In doing so, he would save all who believe in him from the destruction that sin warrants, replacing that condemnation with everlasting life. All who believe will be given this gift. This means absolutely any person, from any background, who puts their trust in him. The apostle Paul summarized this reality perfectly in Galatians 3:28, saying: "There is neither Jew nor Gentile, neither slave nor free, nor is there male and female, for you are all one in Christ Jesus."

All of this reveals an obvious problem. If God is *that* invested in every human being, what about those who existed prior to Christ? More than that, what about those who were neither geographically nor temporally connected to Israel? Were they simply rejected—individuals forsaken as casualties of their times and circumstances? Unfortunately, many of us

---

[176] Zechariah 14:2-4 and Ezekiel 37:24-28 are two good examples of this line of thought.
[177] Isaiah 53 and Zechariah 12:9-14, 13:6-7 are solid examples of this notion.

may believe that is true. Maybe the ancient Sumerians, Egyptians, Aboriginals, and others, were simply born in the wrong place, at the wrong time. Some of us feel that way, but God certainly doesn't.

As previously noted, the Bible most definitely does not support such a vein, arrogant, and ignorant proposition. The apostle Paul even went so far as to clarify that all people—regardless of time period, ethnicity, or geographical location—are capable of understanding and obeying God in their own way. When speaking of the problem with the Gentiles (non-Jews) of ancient times, he had this to say:

> "The wrath of God is being revealed from heaven against all the godlessness and wickedness of people, who suppress the truth by their wickedness, since what may be known about God is plain to them, because God has made it plain to them. For since the creation of the world God's invisible qualities—his eternal power and divine nature—have been clearly seen, being understood from what has been made, so that people are without excuse. For although they knew God, they neither glorified him as God nor gave thanks to him, but their thinking became futile and their foolish hearts were darkened."[178]

Even those who never knew the names Yahweh, Jesus, messiah, or any of the like, *should have* known about God and *should have* been able to revere the Creator according to the witness that was given to them.

The Bible—from top to bottom—reveals that God has great concern for all groups of people, and that concern is not limited to those who have been able to call upon the name of Jesus. *This does not make a knowledgeable rejection of Jesus acceptable.* But it does mean that any Christian who rejects that God was, is, and will forever be interested in reaching out to *all* of His created beings needs to do at least two things. The first is to

---

[178] Romans 1:18-21

stop talking about John 3:16 altogether. You don't really embrace it. The second is to begin reading—*really* reading—the sacred text that we claim is so foundational to our faith. If you believe that God cares more about you than those who lived in ancient Mesopotamia (or elsewhere), then you have completely missed the point. Do not pass Go; do not collect $200. Get off your high horse.

I hope the point is clear. As Christians (or Jews), the belief that God cares for all people is one of the central messages of our sacred Scriptures. It is obvious in both the Old and New Testaments of the Bible. Is this not the very reason why we send missionaries to other countries, or why we participate in any sort of evangelistic (gospel-spreading) practices at all? How strange a thing it is, then, that we so easily dismiss the traditions of how other ancient cultures encountered the "gods" or the "extraterrestrials." Better yet, that we dismiss how those beings made themselves known to these cultures.

Yes, the languages differed. In some respects, the characteristics and descriptions often differed. But I cannot help but wonder if Viracocha, Ahura Mazda, Yahweh, and certain others, are really different entities at all. If we are to agree with the biblical teaching that God has always been in the business of reaching out to the world—the entire world—then we may need to adjust our notions of just how different they really are. If God is truly the God of all, then He could not have simply crossed everyone who lived prior to the Israelites or prior to the time of Jesus off the salvation list.

God had to have made salvation possible to them, just as He has to those who lived during or after the time of Christ. God had to have given them a glimpse into the heavenly realities. Rather than looking at all other ancient religions as being counterfeits of our faith—though some assuredly are—we should begin to investigate the ways that their traditions can add credence to ours. Maybe, just maybe, we may even be able to accept that *certain aspects* of these traditions have always been a part of our own. Perhaps their stories are our stories. If the shoe were on the other foot, I would hope that groups like the Mayans, Incans, or the Aboriginals would not so easily dismiss our claims about a miracle working God-man, whose main purpose on Earth was to get himself killed. Think about it.

A Book like no other

Within this book, I have discussed stories and texts from a wide variety of religious traditions. Among these have been Christianity, Judaism, Hinduism, Buddhism, Islam, and others. As I have made clear throughout the book, there are undeniable parallels that exist among most of the world's prominent religions. Creation stories, flood stories, repeating numbers, the existence of good and evil beings, and so forth, are examples of these parallels. Despite the fact that many people see such comparisons as a threat to the Christian faith—as it somehow makes the Bible less unique—I happen to think the incredible similarities in these traditions further bolster the Bible's claims. I mean, how could all of these separated cultures—both temporally and geographically—share so many commonalties, unless they were all guided (in certain respects, at least) by the same forces?

With this being said, it would be completely irrational to believe that all ancient texts are made the same, or that they are all equally reliable on every issue they discuss. While the overlap between many of the ancient religious traditions is clear, there is a reason why believers hold to the idea that the Bible is the "inspired word of God." This means that God Himself somehow (views vary) collaborated with human authors, in order to produce the texts within the Bible. Yes, there are reasons—and valid reasons, as I will show—why Jews, Christians, and people from other religious (and even non-religious) worldviews believe that the Bible is different: that it is the most important and reliable text of not only the ancient world, but of all time.

While it is often alleged that the Bible is simply a compilation of books that are terribly marred from constant translation and re-translation, that belief is simply false. It has been debunked time and time again, but continues to be a cherished view by those who simply need a reason to deny the Bible's credibility. In reality, biblical translations are not completed by copying the most recent editions, or by appealing to someone's subjective opinion about the meaning of the texts. Instead, our modern translations are created by going back to the source: back to the most ancient texts we have. By referencing those texts—and meticulously comparing them over and against one another—new translations arise.

So, what ancient texts are referenced in this process? How many are involved? The answer to the first question is that the earliest manuscripts are being used in this process. As biblical skeptics are *extremely* quick to point out, a "manuscript" is classified as either a full-length copy of a text or a fragment of a text. Yes, this means that many sources we have from antiquity are bits and pieces of biblical texts. The same applies to every comparable ancient text imaginable. The available manuscripts can vary in categories like the date of writing, who wrote them, the language they used, and the location at which they were written. We have none of the original writings, which are called "autographs." The documents literally penned by the biblical authors, like most other writings from that day and age, were lost to time.

By all professional accounts, there are at least 5,600 Greek manuscripts in existence.[179] Further, there are more than 19,000 additional copies existing in languages like Latin, Syriac, Coptic, and others.[180] This means at least two very important things. First, it means that we have nearly 25,000 total manuscripts of the New Testament, in various languages and from various times. The naysayers will retort to this fact, saying that having tons of manuscripts does not make it true! I have heard this time and time again.

Correct—having more copies of something does not, in and of itself, mean any of it is true. Not only could this be said of every text in

---

[179] See Geisler and Bocchino's, *Unshakeable Foundations*, 256.
[180] See Slick's article, "Manuscript evidence for superior New Testament reliability."

existence, this objection also falls incredibly flat in another sense. Having all of these manuscripts allows us to compare and contrast them, to deduce what might be later additions or faulty translations, and to ascertain what the original content most likely was. It is sort of like having hundreds of testimonies, from many people, as opposed to having only a couple from one or two sources.

When you can compare and contrast a variety of sources, you have a much better basis for determining the actual events. It is difficult to tell if a couple of people are lying about what they saw, but it is much easier to tell who is lying when you have many voices to consider. Certain views are going to line up, exposing those that deviate. In short, having more manuscripts *does* mean that we can be surer of what the original authors intended to say. Like it or not, the manuscripts matter.

This point leads us naturally to the second important thing: our wealth of copies shows us just how little we know about other aspects of ancient history. You know, concerning the types of things that most of us—especially those who doubt the Bible's credibility—take for granted as historical fact. Compare the Bible with other ancient works of the day—many of which I have referenced throughout the book—and this becomes all the more obvious. The writings of the esteemed Greek philosopher, Plato, would have been written between 427-347 BC. What about the earliest copy of his writings? That would date to about 900 AD—more than 1,200 years later. How many copies do we have? Answer: seven.[181] Let's look at Plato's student, Aristotle. His writings would have come from 384-322 BC, but the earliest copy we have of any of them is from about 1100 AD: a separation of 1,400 years or so. Oh yeah, we have only about forty-nine copies of his work.

Clearly, both the dates of the writings and the number of copies are not boding well. What about the second place author and his works? How does the runner-up behind the New Testament fair against it?

---

[181] Ibid.

Homer's epic poem, the *Iliad*, takes the prize. This was generally believed to have been written near 900 BC, and the earliest known manuscript we have is from 400 BC: 500 years later. We know of 643 copies of this text. In full transparency, we know of more than 2,000 copies of all of Homer's works combined, but most are from *far* after the earliest copy.[182] As impressive as the evidence is for Homer's writings, this pales in comparison to the near 25,000 manuscripts of the New Testament, and to the earliest copies we have. The earliest surviving manuscript of the New Testament is Rylands Library Papyrus P52, and it comes from about 125 AD. This is a fragment of the Gospel of John. That would mean the manuscript was written well within a century of the initial autograph (first writing), and perhaps less than thirty years after.[183]

This is not to impugn the credibility of these other works (I tend to trust them), but it does show us that we have much less reason to question the credibility of the Bible, particularly the New Testament (which affirms the Old Testament). The funny thing is, I never hear people question whether or not we can trust the philosophical teachings of Plato or Aristotle, or state that the *Iliad* has been too tampered with to extract its original meaning. We don't hear this about almost anything coming from the ancient world. The Bible appears to be unique in this regard as well. There seems to be a rather prominent agenda to discredit this particular text—the hardest ancient text to ridicule in terms of its historical veracity—and to cast doubt on its reliability. Hmm . . . I simply can't imagine why that would be.

Naturally, others have challenged the notion that our modern biblical translations accurately reflect what was originally recorded (in the autographs). Their reasoning is almost always the same: as time went on, scribes introduced alterations (and errors) into their translations. Like the old "telephone game," the idea is that the more people you

---

[182] See Edwards and Janko's *The Iliad: A Commentary: Volume V*, for more information on this.
[183] See Slick's article, "Manuscript evidence for superior New Testament reliability."

involve, the more errors in the original message that will result. Perhaps most notably, agnostic scholar, Bart Ehrman, has popularized the view that many changes were made to the texts as the translation process progressed over the years. In fact, hundreds of thousands—as many as 400,000—discrepancies are alleged to exist between the many ancient manuscripts.[184]

This assertion is true in some respects, but is also completely false in more important ways. In all, this view is extremely misleading, and the people who make the case know it. The fact is that the *vast* majority of places where different manuscripts vary are absolutely small and meaningless. Most of these variations consist of things like adding a word or letter (particularly the Greek letter ν, or our n), subtracting a word or letter, transposing the order of the words or letters, or substituting a word (often synonymous) or letter. This combination of variations are said, by some, to have made the Bible into an error-ridden collection of books.

Textual critic and professor, Dr. Maurice Robinson, ran a test to see just how often meaningful changes were *really* made in any of these aspects.[185] In order to do so, he took thirty random manuscripts (or, MSS) from the 2nd and 3rd centuries AD, an era proposed (by Ehrman and others) to have seen a great increase in textual variations. He compared those manuscripts against what is called the Byzantine Textform. The reason why this was a good comparison is that none of those texts are known to have arisen earlier than the middle of the 4th century AD, so they are able to compare a good cross range of texts. As Robinson said, "the amount of textual diversity and divergence should be maximized in such a test."[186] Each of these manuscripts contained at least five passages, and he compared them based on the known

---

[184] Ehrman makes claims like this all throughout his book, *Misquoting Jesus*.
[185] This is recorded in Tom Howe's paper, "A Reponse to Bart D. Ehrman's *Misquoting Jesus*," 17-19.
[186] Ibid.

variations above (addition, subtraction, transposition, and substitution). He used Matthew 13, Acts 13, Romans 13, Hebrews 13, and Revelation 13.

Robinson found that there is a 92.2% average stability in the text during the time when the largest number of variants are alleged to have arisen. Robinson summarized what this means quite well:

> "The present experiment has shown that the text as a whole remains remarkably consistent — not merely between the early papyri and the text of the fourth century manuscripts, but between the early papyri and the text found in manuscripts dating more than 1,000 years later. Indeed, the base form of the autograph text has been substantially preserved, tending to differ only in minor details among the manuscripts. The primary base text otherwise clearly represents that which originally had been given by the sacred writers in the first century."[187]

We just don't see the legitimate changes that are alleged to have occurred over the centuries of translation and transmission. No one is denying that there are *differences* within the thousands of New Testament manuscripts, or that there are zero authentic discussions to be had. But no one should be arguing that the translations we have today have been radically, or even significantly, altered from the texts that were originally written. That is a baseless and disingenuous charge, and it needs to stop.

The fact that most of the differences between manuscripts are petty and singularly insignificant has not even escaped people like Ehrman, who have attempted to at least project something to the contrary. In an interview included in the appendix of *Misquoting Jesus*, Ehrman makes an astonishing admission when reflecting on the work of the esteemed textual scholar (and his own mentor), Bruce Metzger:

---

[187] Maurice Robinson, "The Integrity of the Early New Testament Text."

> "If he and I were put in a room and asked to hammer out a consensus statement on what we think the original text of the New Testament probably looked like, there would be very few points of disagreement – maybe one or two dozen places out of many thousands. The position I argue for in 'Misquoting Jesus' does not actually stand at odds with Prof. Metzger's position that the essential Christian beliefs are not affected by textual variants in the manuscript tradition of the New Testament."[188]

In essence, Ehrman admits that the essential teachings within the Bible *have not* been altered through the transmission of its manuscripts, and that any differences would be both rare and minor. This is exactly what one might expect from someone who also wrote a book about how the Bible cannot provide a good explanation for human suffering, only to adopt a biblical view on the matter himself![189] Still, this is evidence that the charges of biblical tampering and unreliability have been way overblown, if not outright fabricated.

Just to provide a final piece of evidence as to why the biblical texts should be trusted—in terms of what they were meant to say, if nothing else—consider the book of Isaiah. Until 1947, the only full-length copy (or close) we possessed of this book came from 1008 AD.[190] The change in that year was brought to us through an archaeological goldmine, called the Dead Sea Scrolls. Among the many revolutionary discoveries that came in 1946-1947 was a copy of the book of Isaiah, which was dubbed the "Great Isaiah Scroll." The Great Isaiah Scroll (or simply, the Isaiah

---

[188] Ibid. 252

[189] This occurred in the book, *God's Problem*. The purpose of the book was to show that the Bible does not provide an adequate answer to the issue of human suffering. However, Ehrman ends up agreeing with the way the book of Ecclesiastes handles the issue. As Ehrman said, "I have to admit that at the end of the day, I do have a biblical view of suffering. As it turns out, it is the view put forth in the book of Ecclesiastes." See pages 276-78.

[190] See Sean McDowell, "What are the Dead Sea Scrolls and Why Do They Matter?"

Scroll) is an almost completely intact copy of the book of Isaiah—which is an extremely large text—and it dates to around 125 BC.[191]

As with any ancient text, there were of course minor differences and spelling changes; the two texts were over 1,100 years apart, after all. But no honest scholar would suggest that the two texts differed in any significant way. For all intents and purposes, a sixty-six chapter text (as we have it) had been translated over and over again for more than a millennium, and remained virtually unchanged. Both of these copies would deliver the same information about God, and His workings in the world. So much for the idea that the copying and translating processes wrecked the Bible.

With all of this being said, there are certainly a significant number of people who continue to treat the Bible like a mistake-laden book, replete with frauds and counterfeit teachings about history. It is an easy (and false) way to dismiss a text that spiritually challenges all of us in tremendous ways. Very well. As Jesus once said, "many are called and few are chosen" (Mt. 22:14). For some people—particularly those who simply do not want to believe that the Bible could be telling the truth—there will never be enough evidence. Ever. But there is an unmistakable and irrefutable reality that people of this stripe must come to terms with, and Christian apologists have rightly been touting it for decades now: if you dismiss the biblical texts because they are somehow "historically unreliable," then you must—absolutely and unequivocally *must*—dismiss every other text from ancient history. There are no two ways about it.

We would have to throw out the *Epic of Gilgamesh*, the *Book of the Dead*, the *Atra-Hasis*, Homer's *Iliad* and *Odyssey*, and every single thing ever recorded about an ancient king or his respective kingdom. There was no Alexander the Great, Marcus Aurelius, Emperor Nero, or anyone else. If there was, why would we trust a single thing that was recorded about them? None of these examples have even a fraction of the available writings and historical validation that Jesus, Paul, and most of the other

---

[191] Ibid.

biblical figures have. I am certainly not advocating this type of distrust in human history, but it is necessary for anyone who dismisses the historicity of the biblical accounts. This is even true for the miraculous occurrences, not just the mundane references to things like ancient locations and the existence of particular individuals. If you can trust the historical statements of the Bible, it seems *extremely* selective to believe that all the "magical parts"—as skeptics love to call them—are made up.

This is why the Bible is a book like no other. It is the most scrutinized, printed, read, researched, distributed, and influential text in all of world history, and there is no close second. On top of that, it has been verified by all manner of scholars (even skeptics) that no essential changes were made to the biblical manuscripts over the course of more than 2,000 years of transmission. While I certainly advocate that other ancient texts and traditions carry a great deal of value and truth—and that they can often reveal the ways in which God has reached out to the world—it should be obvious that the Bible must be placed on a pedestal of its own. Further, we can have great confidence that when the Bible tells us something happened, it can be taken on excellent authority that it actually did. Since the Bible clearly talks about beings of higher power, it may well be the best source of evidence for "aliens" (and the Being who created them) in all of existence.

That Kind of Creator

If I—and many millions of other believers throughout history—am right about the Bible, and it really is a book like no other, then we simply must ask about the God of this extraordinary text. What is this God like? Is He good, evil, benevolent, malevolent, or what? If you recall, I actually began to discuss this issue very early on; I wanted to set the stage right away for what is probably the most important issue of the book, and perhaps of all reality. You may also remember that I discussed a science fiction film I had watched, while on a fishing trip with my father and brother. The title of the film was *Prometheus*, and the concepts it presented sent a shiver down my spine. Though I chose not to disclose more about it at the beginning of the book, the time has now come to do so.

Prometheus is a story about a group of human beings who have reason to believe that they might be able to answer two of life's most ancient (and crucial) questions: *why* are we here, and *how* did we get here? On their ship—which is of course called the "Prometheus"—the crew travels a long way across the universe in an attempt to track down the beings (dubbed "engineers") who made them. When they finally explore the planet they were searching for, they find things that none of them could ever have expected. Strange creatures attack them, and some even fall victim to this threat in very brutal ways. However, the ship's leaders ultimately meet one of the beings they were looking for; they find one of humanity's creators.

Though the others had either become deceased or had long-since vanished, one of these "gods" remained in some form of cryogenic state. When they wake him from his slumber, he is none too happy about seeing these pesky humans stand before him. In fact, this humanoid figure is *anything* but friendly or inviting. Instead, it kills several of them, tears the head off of the crew's android guide (David), and then sets its sights on coming to Earth in order to get rid of its inhabitants. As it turned out, humanity was disposable. This being did not see us as its precious little children, as the pinnacle of its creation, or anything of the sort. Quite the contrary; we were actually a "failed experiment" that no longer deserved to occupy a single star in an otherwise enormous universe.

In a very real sense, the being who was responsible for humanity's existence in the movie is the very type of being proposed by ancient astronaut theorists and others. This "engineer" lived on another planet within the universe. It was *somewhat* humanoid. It had advanced crafts that allowed it to travel through space. It had, at some point, ventured to Earth and seeded life on this planet. Afterwards, it vanished, and essentially made no concrete appearances or provided any genuine self-disclosures.

Most importantly—and what ends up being one of the major twists of the movie—the being that the crew had so fiercely encountered was not the top of the food chain. While some believed they were going to encounter the real Creator—"God," in the truest sense—they were not. Quite the contrary: they had only found the next being up on the totem pole. This created a spiritual dilemma for the movie's main character, Elizabeth Shaw. Being cast as a Christian researcher, the discovery of this type of creator puzzled her greatly. Her co-researcher and romantic partner, Charlie Holloway, remarked that she should take her "father's cross off now." When Elizabeth asks him why she should do that, his reasoning was simple: "Because they made us." They had discovered "God," and it was not Jesus Christ.

After this exchange, Elizabeth had a zinging (but perhaps, obvious) response of her own: "And who made them?" Yes, that creature had made human beings . . . but another creature had made that creature. To her, the existence of an entity of greater stature (the engineers) did not eliminate the need for one that had not been created (God). She got it; she understood. By the end of the film, Dr. Elizabeth Shaw (the lone survivor) was setting out to understand why her creators wanted to destroy humanity, and also to find *the being/s who made* their creators. If you recall the earlier section about abiogenesis—how life ever came to exist in the first place—this should sound eerily familiar.

While Elizabeth was right that an uncaused Creator is the only thing that could properly describe our existence (though it was not directly stated), her spiritual dilemma poses powerful questions to us. While entities like the "engineers" would share important similarities with God and the angelic beings—like creative ability, embodiment, transportation, and some physical resemblance to human beings—they are not a great deal like the God of Christianity or Judaism. There are some very stark contrasts between the *Prometheus* engineer and the biblical Creator. From front to back, the Bible portrays God as having an incomprehensible care and affection for His created beings. Clearly, this was not something the engineers possessed.

Though it is undeniable that God destroyed human beings at times, particularly with the Flood, He did so because of continued human disobedience and rejection: "Then the Lord saw that the wickedness of man was great on the earth, and that every intent of the thoughts of his heart was only evil continually" (Gen. 6:5). More than that, it is often said that events like the Flood grieved God, much more (I believe) than we are able to imagine. The NLT translates God's feelings about human disobedience before the Flood very well: "So the LORD was sorry he had ever made them and put them on the earth. It broke his heart" (Gen. 6:6).

The most important thing we learn about God's concern for humanity is found in the very beginning: God made us in His image, and according to His own likeness (Gen. 1:26). While I will not go into incredible detail about what all that really encompasses, suffice it to say that we are *very* much like God. We are not identical, but very similar. I believe there is both a physical and spiritual connotation to this. We have emotions like anger, joy, sorrow, disgust, and many others. So does God. We live in communion with others, but have our own identities. So does God. We are tangible entities. So is God (recall the previous section, "physical beings"). Notice also that we were the last creature to be created by God; we were undoubtedly the climax of everything He ever made on Earth.

The Bible records the great lengths to which God went in reaching out to humanity, and to save us from ourselves. Through Satan and human disobedience, sin and separation entered the world (Gen. 3). God very well could have called the whole thing off at that point, and He of course would have been within His rights to do so. But He did not. Instead, He immediately chose to fix the problem that had just been created; "I will put enmity Between you and the woman, And between your seed and her seed; He shall bruise you on the head, And you shall bruise him on the heel" (3:15). In other words, a human being would ultimately crush the serpent that had deceived them, and life would go on.

God reached another pivotal point soon afterwards in Genesis, when humanity had become incredibly corrupt and the Nephilim (the "giants" discussed in chapter three) were roaming the Earth. God would have been within His rights to stop the project at that point also, but decided to preserve a remnant (Noah and his family) in order to propagate the human race (Gen. 6). Sadly, God faced this dilemma yet again, as soon as humanity had actually begun to flourish after the Flood. The new society decided to erect a mammoth tower in order to glorify themselves, rather than the God who had created them: "let us build for ourselves a city . . . and let us make for ourselves a name" (Gen. 11:4). Here again, God could very well have cashed out and put an end to the whole human project. Instead, He chose life. God scattered the people and confused their languages, in the hopes that something may change in them. Of course, it ultimately did not change. Fallen human beings continued to be, well, fallen human beings.

This type of thing occurred throughout the *entire* time period recorded in the Old Testament. In essence, the Old Testament is a tragic story of human disobedience, and God's perseverance. Perhaps the most poignant example of this fact is the age of the "judges" in Israel. That era can be summarized just as the last verse (and others throughout) of the entire book of Judges suggests: "In those days there was no king in Israel; everyone did what was right in his own eyes" (21:25). This concluding statement does two things. First, it alludes to the belief that, somehow, having a human king would make everything better. As one follows the succession of Israelite Kings (beginning with Saul) through the rest of the historical books and the prophets, it is crystal clear that such a thing was nothing more than a pipe dream; many of them proved to be corrupt to the core. Second, it does show us that, by their own admission, Israel was a very disobedient nation. They came nowhere near living up to the covenant that God had made with their ancestors through Moses (Ex. 19-24, Dt. 29).

It has long been taught that the book of Judges—which is titled because of the series of military/legal rulers (judges) that governed Israel for a time—followed a continuous pattern. The people would sin, then suffer the consequences, then repent (temporarily, of course), and finally God would restore them by raising up a new judge. This was a time wrought with political strife and corruption. The nation would rebound or prosper under judges like Samson, Gideon, and Deborah, only to sink into complete immorality again and again. Sadly, that same cycle would have applied throughout the entire Old Testament narrative.

Even when God permitted them to have kings, the vicious pattern continued. For every David or Hezekiah, there was a Saul or an Ahaz, and even the greatest of kings (like David himself) committed terrible sins and had moments of complete failure (2 Sam. 11). On top of all this, I already discussed the exile,[192] which was really the end result of all Israel's unfaithfulness. Yet, God caused the Persian king, Cyrus, to send them back home so they could rebuild and try again (Ezra 1).

Clearly, God's patience was not infinite, and many of *His own* people suffered the ultimate penalty for their behavior. The point is that God showed an incredible care to keep humanity going, and to solve the problem of human sin and suffering. When the people continued to throw God lemons, He continued to make lemontinis. God could have stepped in to eradicate the entire mess of us, at any point, and even we as human beings could hardly have blamed Him! It is literally mind-boggling how persistent the God of the Bible is.

Along the way, God made Himself known to the people in tremendous ways. He appeared to Moses through a burning bush (Ex. 3). He led the Israelites across the wilderness through pillars of fire and smoke (Ex. 13:21). He appeared through a whirlwind (Job 38:1). God also showed up

---

[192] See the earlier section, "God of All," for further explanation of the exile.

to the prophet Ezekiel in a mysterious flying craft (Ez. 1), just like the angels did to others (2 Ki. 2). One of my personal favorites is when God literally showed Himself—as He typically exists (i.e. the "norm")—to Moses, upon his request (Ex. 33:18-23). God also "wrestled" with Jacob for most of an entire evening (Gen. 32:22-32).

God created the world, but did not depart and leave us alone. Even when we tried to make Him do so, He did not. When Adam and Eve rebelled, God promised redemption. When humanity had become incredibly evil, God spared Noah and his family in order to start new. When the era of judges and kings failed, God promised a perfect ruler: a shepherd who would righteously rule the sheep. After Israel's disobedience led her into exile, God worked through a pagan emperor to bring His people home again. You can scarcely fabricate the kind of human failure that God has pushed through! None of this includes the utter lack of belief Jesus' followers often showed him, or the fact that he was betrayed by one of his own apostles (Judas). If you were creating a religion, these sorts of things would not be the foundation you would want to start with; it's not how you would try to write it up. Unless, of course, all of this actually happened. The Bible is brutally honest—and thus, quite believable—about the nature of human beings and the atrocities we have committed.

It is equally emphatic that Yahweh has reached out to the world—the *whole world*. If you could speak with the ancient Chinese, the Mayans, the Assyrians, or any of the like, they would have their own stories about how God contacted them too. Some are undoubtedly fictitious, or were even misconstrued examples of demonic influence. But many were undoubtedly not. As I discussed in the previous sections, God has always been in the business of communicating with all of His created beings.

In the process of doing so, God did things that no higher life form on some distant planet could ever have accomplished: some typical "alien," or the engineers. Causing a massive flood, speaking through flaming vegetation, utilizing pillars of fire, and so much more, were standard ways that God reached out to the people in Old Testament times. In certain respects—

and as hard as it may be to believe or understand—these examples pale in comparison to God's most impressive self-disclosure. The promise given to Adam and Eve, which ran throughout the entire Old Testament, finally came to fruition. God decided to take care of the human dilemma by throwing Himself directly into the fray. The result would change history forever.

The Ultimate Extraterrestrial

In the process of reaching out to the world, the Bible describes many ways that God physically interacted with human beings. Some readers may be thinking that I have failed to mention the most incredible way that God reached out to humanity, and the most powerful expression of His feelings towards us. He is known as the "son of man," the "lamb of God," "the Christ," the "alpha and the omega," and by many other names. Most of us simply know him as Jesus, and he stands out above every known figure in human history. Even those who reject that he was anything more than a famous man—a fact which virtually no serious historian can dispute—would not attempt to disagree that Jesus holds a unique place within the story of humanity. Make no mistake about it: to those who believe in the existence of a higher power (which is *most* of us, and always has been), Jesus can be seen as the ultimate extraterrestrial.

While the ancient astronaut crowd has shown hesitation (for whatever reason) in calling Jesus an "alien,"[193] there is an undeniable sense in which he is one. He is not from another planet within the universe—which is probably, among other reasons I will mention, part of why ancient astronaut theorists do not classify him as an alien—but he is certainly alien to our world. In some respects, at least. One of the most intriguing things about Jesus is that he is both an "extraterrestrial" and a

---

[193] While using other biblical examples to suggest the existence of extraterrestrials, such as Ezekiel's vision, Jesus never seems to be mentioned in the same way. See Jason Colavito's article, "Ancient Astronaut Hypocrisy," for an example of this conundrum.

"terrestrial." He is from heaven, but he was also bound to Earth. He lived apart from us, yet he lived here as one of us.

This means that Jesus is not just another in the line of beings who visited the world. He is not merely a created entity, or some underling that must report back to its maker. Jesus is the Maker. Jesus is the one to whom others report. And that very same person—before he became the man Jesus—was the one who created life on Earth, and humanity itself. After humanity—and let's not forget, the "sons of God" and the Nephilim also—made a mess of this world, he was also ultimately the one who came to clean up the disaster. The Creator became one of the created, in order to rectify our atrocities. More than that, Jesus allowed the very ones he came to save to murder him in horrific fashion.

But before Jesus gave his life on a miserable Roman cross, quite a lot happened. So much, in fact, that one of his closest friends and followers wrote this at the end of his account of Jesus' life: "And there are also many other things which Jesus did, which if they were written in detail, I suppose that even the world itself would not contain the books that would be written" (Jn. 21:25). One might feel like that is a stretch—particularly because Jesus' ministry probably only lasted about three years (at most)—but it is not.

For that entire period of time, Jesus performed one astonishing miracle after another. This was God's ultimate display of evidence: of "proof," if you will. All of the times He had reached out to the world through visions, visitations, architectural achievements, flying machines, pillars of fire, catastrophic events, and all of the like, were signals pointing towards a time when He would personally grace us with His presence. Jesus was it; he was the way that God chose to fully reveal both Himself and His power to the world. And Jesus did not disappoint.

While we know virtually nothing about Jesus as a child—except that he once taught at the temple when he was twelve (Lk. 2:41-52)—we sure see a lot of him after it was time to begin his mission. I previously discussed the issue of human possession, and how it is an example of how extraterrestrial beings (demons, in this case) interact in our world. Speaking of which, Jesus first burst onto the scene as the master exorcist. In the Gospel of Mark, it is clear that Jesus first rose in popularity because he was able to cast out demons in shocking fashion. One of the very earliest events that occurred in Jesus' ministry—assuming that Mark really was the first gospel to be written—involved him casting out a demon in a place called Capernaum. No sooner does Jesus walk into the local synagogue, that a demon-possessed man starts berating him. After effortlessly dispatching the demon, Mark 1:27-28 records the following:

> "They were all amazed, so that they debated among themselves, saying, 'What is this? A new teaching with authority! He commands even the unclean spirits, and they obey Him.' Immediately the news about Him spread everywhere into all the surrounding district of Galilee."

From there, Jesus went on to cast demons out of both children and adults on at least seven or eight different occasions. And that's just what was recorded in the New Testament. Clearly, it was a regular part of his ministry. Jesus also made it known that it would be a regular part of his disciples' ministry, as well (Mk. 16:17). Exorcisms were by no stretch his only supernatural skill, either. Another popular activity for Jesus was to heal sick people. In fact, stricken members of society would come from all over in the hopes of being healed. Among other things, Jesus succeeded in curing blindness (Mk. 10-52, Jn. 9:1-12), leprosy (Mt. 8:1-4), paralysis (Mk. 2:1-12), and edema (Lk. 14:1-6). Jesus was able to heal a man with no personal contact, who was—at that exact time—a great distance away from him (Jn. 4:46-54). This should not be the slightest bit surprising, since Jesus was also able to bring people back from the dead at will.[194] He even had power over life and death!

---

[194] It is recorded that Jesus raised Lazarus (Jn. 11:1-44), Jairus' daughter (Mk. 5:21-43), and a man from Nain (Lk. 7:11-17) back to life.

These are just a few of Jesus' amazing feats. On one occasion, he was able to instantly change the chemical makeup of water. In one of his most famous miracles, he turned water into wine at a wedding reception in a place called Cana (Jn. 2:1-11). There, Jesus told the servants to pour plain old H20 into large stone jars. Somewhere between the time it was being poured and the time it had reached the master of the feast's lips, the simple water had turned into world-class wine. In all, he may have made up to 180 gallons of wine at that moment.[195] I don't know about you, but I want to go to one of Jesus' parties!

Jesus was no stranger to manipulating water, either. While the term "walking on water" has come to refer to people who think they are something special, it is based on someone who really was special. The next example occurred alongside of another of Jesus' miracles—the "Feeding of the 5,000"—in which Jesus desired to be left alone for a bit in order to pray. The disciples decided to go ahead of Jesus, and Matthew 14:24-26 records the following:

> "But the boat was already a long distance from the land, battered by the waves; for the wind was contrary. And in the fourth watch of the night He came to them, walking on the sea. When the disciples saw Him walking on the sea, they were terrified, and said, 'It is a ghost!' And they cried out in fear."

From a great distance away, Jesus simply strolled across the Sea of Galilee in order to reach their boat. Upon seeing what Jesus was doing, the ever-spontaneous Peter decides to hop down into the water himself. Amazingly, Peter was actually able to walk across the water as well, until he stopped to think about how crazy the whole thing was. Jesus demonstrated that he could walk on water, and cause others to do so as well.

---

[195] There were six stone jars in all. Each was filled to the brim, and held as much as thirty gallons of water. Do the math.

Jesus was not quite finished yet with his aquatic demonstrations. On another occasion, Jesus was out on the sea with his disciples, and a wicked storm kicked up out of nowhere: "And there arose a fierce gale of wind, and the waves were breaking over the boat so much that the boat was already filling up" (Mk. 4:37). In the stern section, an utterly exhausted Jesus somehow remained asleep during the raucous event, at least until his horrified disciples came to wake him up. How typical of them.

Almost annoyed, Jesus stands up and instantly puts a stop to the pesky storm, saying, "Hush, be still" (Mk. 4:39). The wind died down, and the sea went calm as glass. The most interesting thing is that the disciples became even more afraid *after* the storm had stopped. This time, they were terrified of Jesus himself: "They became very much afraid and said to one another, 'Who then is this, that even the wind and the sea obey Him'?" (Mk. 4:41). If you think about it, it was only reasonable to fear Jesus in that moment. How could anyone control the weather?

In Jesus' final act, he showed us something truly astonishing: what *we* will one day be like. This is something that many self-proclaimed Christians don't even know about (it is rarely taught, for some reason), but Jesus rose from the dead in a very unique way. As if coming back to life was not enough, Jesus returned from the grave with a new body—a body that was quite different than the one he previously had, or that we now possess. After the Resurrection, two things stand out above the other important realities. The first is that Jesus was physically unrecognizable.

On one occasion, two of his disciples walked and talked with Jesus for roughly seven miles, and never recognized that it was him the entire time (Lk. 24:13-35). There was another event where Jesus appeared to the disciples while they were out fishing on the Sea of Galilee (Jn. 21:1-14). First, they did not recognize Jesus when he called to them from the shore, even though he was clearly close enough to recognize (about 100 yards away). More astonishingly, they still had doubts about his identity even after reaching the shore and sitting down to eat with him (Jn. 21:12). In fact, the apostles—who were his closest followers—were almost never able to physically recognize him on the occasions he appeared to them after the Resurrection. They were only tipped off by his characteristics and actions.

It is important to note something here. Even though Jesus was changed, he did not appear as some type of completely non-human entity. He was not physically recognizable, but no one reported that he looked like a different type of creature. In fact, Mary Magdalene—on what was probably a passing glance—thought he was the gardener (Jn. 20:15). The implication is that Jesus at least resembled someone who was human. Heavenly beings are not identical to human beings, but they are clearly quite similar. Throughout the Bible, angels appear to us in like manner.[196]

The second major thing the Resurrection proved was that we will also have that type of body someday. The apostle Paul spent a great deal of time speaking about this point. When talking about Jesus' resurrection body (and our future bodies), Paul said the following:

> "What comes first is the natural body, then the spiritual body comes later. Adam, the first man, was made from the dust of the earth, while Christ, the second man, came from heaven. Earthly people are like the earthly man, and heavenly people are like the heavenly man. Just as we are now like the earthly man, we will someday be like the heavenly man" (1 Cor. 15:46-49, NLT).

I mentioned this passage a little earlier, since it shows that heavenly beings have bodies. In the present discussion, the implication is pretty clear: human beings currently have bodies like the one Adam was created with, but we will someday have bodies like the one Jesus was raised from the dead with. Further, Jesus said that we will be like the angels at the resurrection (Mt. 22:30). Jesus' resurrection body is similar in type to the

---

[196] For just a few examples, see Genesis 19:1-29, John 20:11-15, and Hebrews 13:2. We *always* see angels appear as beings resembling human form throughout the Bible. This is because they are similar to us, in many respects.

kind the angels have, and we will ultimately join them all in that type of existence.

All of these amazing events are just a small portion of what Jesus was able to accomplish. As previously noted, the Gospel of John states that the world could not contain all of the books containing Jesus' miracles, if they had all been chronicled (Jn. 21:25). That may contain a touch of hyperbole, but only a touch. Healing the blind, the paralyzed, and all manner of sick people—check. Having the power to bring dead people back to life and restore animation—check. Raising oneself from the dead—check. Stopping the wind, the waves, and the weather in general—check. Producing a wonderful Cabernet Sauvignon (est. 30 AD)—double check. Indeed, all of this points to a special type of power and ability.

But that's just it: these feats were brought about by incredible power. One might even say they came—as the popular hymn says—through "pow'r, pow'r, wonder-working pow'r!" Jesus shows us something important about the "extraterrestrials" or "aliens" we have been looking at throughout this book. Things like curing sick or dead people from a distance, driving out demonic forces, controlling the weather, and so on, are not the products of just being more intelligently advanced than we are. It's not a matter of being around longer than us, or having the time and ability to make better technology. Jesus never used anything of the sort.

As I have suggested all along, being "smarter" or "more evolved" cannot account for most of what is attributed to beings of higher intelligence. At what point does a being become so intelligent that it can stop the weather with a word? What type of technology allows someone to layer the universe with mathematical equations, and make it function according to them? How much more "advanced" must one be in order to flood the Earth, or at least huge portions of it? Who knows, maybe with a few hundred more years of *alleged* human evolution, we will be able to shout at tombs and have dead people emerge from them! You may see where I am going with this. A more advanced being, who has just persisted longer than we have, could not account for all we see happening. The visitors proposed by ancient astronaut theorists would fall short in too many important ways. Jesus shows us that, to be sure.

All of this means that Jesus is, without question, the ultimate extraterrestrial. He was an extraterrestrial who became a terrestrial, without ceasing to be the former. He showed us a glimpse into the world of the divine that is absolutely without parallel. He showed us the power of God through miracles. He showed us the character of God in his dealings with all manner of people. He showed us what it's like to die with dignity. Lastly, he also showed us a glimpse into the future of our world. One day, we will be like Jesus in form (not in divinity). We will all be aliens.

God Made the Aliens

In this final section, I want to briefly recap the most important ideas that have been presented, and bring the book to a logical conclusion. Hopefully, this will help to drive home the major points I have discussed, while also leaving the reader some things to really ponder. The first set of realities to summarize provides evidence that *some* other beings, who exist *somewhere* else, have reached out to the world. That belief is certainly necessary, if we are to worry about understanding the identities of these beings or anything else. That is actually the second task of this section: to describe the evidence I offered that will help us to understand what type of entities best account for extraterrestrial contact. Lastly, I want to briefly explain why a belief in angelic beings—rather than a typical "alien" who lives somewhere else in the cosmos—makes the best sense of things as a whole. The angels are the aliens.

We began our journey talking about what may actually be the most taboo topic in the book: UFOs. While many are fascinated by this phenomenon, there can be little doubt that any discussion of it can result in an instant dismissal by others. Worse, some people will all but throw a tinfoil hat on you, just for entertaining something so preposterous. This may be especially true within the church, actually. But as I said at the onset, there is simply too much evidence at this point to dismiss it. I talked about some of the most incredible examples of UFO interactions, many involving extremely credible people (like airline pilots and former NASA employees). In fact, some people who have testified to seeing a UFO have much to lose by doing so. People with a lot to lose make very poor liars, particularly when they take a position that is anathema (accursed) to their co-workers or superiors.

Besides all of this, I am not a big fan of calling hundreds of thousands of people deceivers about what they have seen. There is no question that many UFO events have been either made up or highly fabricated, but there is no way that *all* of them have been. For my part, I have even seen at least one UFO in my life, and I would bet the farm that the craft was not man-made. Of course, there is also the reality that the Bible clearly discusses the types of crafts often described in UFO sightings. Elijah was carried off on one, Ezekiel was visited by one, and Elisha and his servant saw scores of them on the mountain. For people of faith in particular, it does not seem very forthright to jettison all of this, chalking it up to superstition or efforts to obtain recognition. By all accounts we could consider, UFOs exist.

In my mind, the same beings who pilot UFOs also appeared to many of the ancient cultures in history. As I mentioned, some were well-intentioned, and others probably were not. The same applies to anything related to angelic beings. Whatever the case, beings of higher intelligence continue to be the best explanation for the advanced architecture of the ancient world. When 21st century engineers cannot tell us how buildings made more than four millennia ago were constructed, that should be a pretty good indication that they had help. Lifting blocks that are in excess of 2-tons, to heights exceeding 450 feet—as we see in the Great Pyramid—is scarcely a feasible activity by *today's* standards, much less by theirs. I don't know how our extraterrestrial visitors did it, either. But I don't need an explanation *for* the explanation in this case. There appeared to be—based on the evidence we do have—a power or technological understanding that exceeds our own at work in things like the Giza pyramid complex. That much we can tell.

More than that, we know that these structures often correspond with the celestial bodies. The Mayan temple structure at Tikal directly corresponds with the Pleiades constellation, which is where the "sky beings" who made them were thought to have come from. We also saw that the three largest pyramids at Giza, the Hopi Mesas, and the pyramid complex in Teotihuacán all align with Orion's Belt. This means that ancient cultures in Egypt, North America, and Mexico shared an obsession with the same cluster of stars, and developed eerily similar architecture accordingly. A strange coincidence, I suppose.

Other "coincidences" that were evaluated include the incredible similarities that exist among ancient creation accounts. The Babylonian *Enuma Elish*, the Norse cosmogony, many of the ancient Chinese creation stories, and of course, the Bible, all essentially confirm that our world was brought forth out of chaos and turned into order by a divine being (or beings). In some cases, even the exact order of creation was the same: first came plant life, next came animal life, and then finally, human beings were created. From there, it was very well-established that flood stories pervaded almost every culture imaginable. Within these stories, divine beings were responsible for a catastrophic flood, typically due to dissatisfaction with the behavior of the human race.

Naturally, there is a great deal of science that would support the notion of a Great Flood. Well-respected researchers have noted the evidence of floods from around the world, particularly in the Middle East. Further, the existence of marine fossils all over the Earth—from our deserts, to the summit of Mt. Everest—is undeniable. The explanation that these fossils were deposited hundreds of millions of years ago, and were then elevated as mountains rose from beneath the sea, is so incredibly speculative that no one should be suggesting it. It requires unverified assumptions about the evolution of the animals that left the remains, when and how the great mountain ranges came to exist, our carbon dating techniques, and much more. That is simply the required story, in order to try to explain the evidence naturalistically. The most obvious and reasonable explanation is that water once covered these areas, *after* both the mountain ranges and the diversity of species on them (found in the fossil remains) came to exist.

Then there was the second part of the evidence—the strange collection of phenomena that point specifically to extraterrestrial entities. Along the way, it became clear that the "aliens" of the ancient astronaut perspective could not have been responsible for all of these examples. To the ancients, there was a battle between good and evil occurring all around (and among) us. We saw this with Zoroastrianism's Ahura Mazda and the Evil Spirit Ahriman, with Islam's Allah, Shaitan and the djinni, and of course with Yahweh, Satan, and the angelic beings of the Bible. The countless possession accounts in history align well with this type of spiritual warfare.

Like these possession accounts, the incidences of spontaneous human combustion (SHC) that have been chronicled also point to the existence of non-human entities. Michael Faherty, Mary Hardy Reeser ("The Cinder Lady"), John Irving Bentley, and the other examples mentioned, show that occurrences like those in the book of Job and at Sodom and Gomorrah are not just mythological history; they still happen. This is another example of something that, while extremely odd, has been documented without any suitable scientific explanation. People really have caught on fire for no known reason, and some unfortunate souls have been burnt to ash.

The issues of possession and spontaneous human combustion really began the process of forcing us to ask second-level questions about the nature of the beings responsible for the events. This was the third, and final, piece of the book. Like the construction of the Egyptian pyramids, the Mayan knowledge of astronomy, and so many other things, the best explanation going is that extraterrestrials (non-human entities from somewhere other than Earth) are responsible. But the question that has been posed throughout this book is, what *kind* of extraterrestrials are we talking about? My suggestion has been that it makes sense to believe in entities that do not have to traverse the universe in order to influence us. By this, I mean something closer to the biblical understanding of God and the angels: beings who are not confined to our world or universe, who have incredible power and intelligence, and do not have to travel across space to get here.

There are certainly similarities between the beings proposed by ancient astronaut theorists (like on *Ancient Aliens*) and the heavenly beings of the Bible. In fact, there are more similarities than many theists might want to believe. In particular, the tangible nature of the heavenly beings is something the ancient astronaut theorists have right; the Bible clearly tells us that angels, and even the resurrected Jesus, exist in physical form. They are also right in the general premise that intelligent beings from somewhere other than Earth— "extraterrestrials," in the most literal sense—are the very best explanation for our existence and the world around us. Many authors from that background have provided exceptional evidence for this idea, and I have underlined some of these reasons within this book.

On the other hand, the extraterrestrials offered up in ancient astronaut theory (AAT) simply cannot explain, in principle, all of the phenomena we see. The "engineers" I discussed from the movie *Prometheus* are quite similar to the beings put forth in AAT. The engineers are extraterrestrials who ventured through the universe in a giant spaceship, seeded life on Earth, and then abruptly flew back to their planet. This is problematic for two major reasons. The first is that these beings could not have accomplished things like possession, spontaneous human combustion (SHC), the miracles Jesus performed, and the origin of life in the universe. I will explain the latter of these momentarily. Both SHC and possession would absolutely require beings that are present among the victims. In order to take control of someone, or to cause them to burn up, the entity would need to be close enough to do it. This also means that the entity, if from another planet, would need to travel here; they would be seen in their transit, or at least seen during the event itself.

The miracles that Jesus performed are out of reach for these types of extraterrestrials too, but for different reasons. Jesus turned water into wine, cast out demons, manipulated the weather, brought dead people back to life, and so many other things. None of this—I repeat, *none of this*—has anything to do with simply being smarter than we are, or being more "evolved" than us. It has only to do with power. Jesus had a power that could never be achieved through more time, more understanding, or any of the like. He certainly had those capacities, but he clearly had something more. Again, at what point would we suddenly develop the ability to walk on water, change its chemical composition with a few words, or call a dead person out of the grave? Enough said.

Perhaps the most undeniable example is found in the issue of abiogenesis, or how life could have emerged from non-life in the first place. As I pointed out in the section, "A Crick Word about the Origin of Life," the typical definition of an alien just wouldn't suffice to explain how life exists in the universe. Even if there are beings that live somewhere else within the universe, they must also have been engineered. If our existence is best explained by an intelligent cause, then so is theirs. If we have no idea how life could have begun here, we cannot simply punt the problem off to the next star. Given the complete lack of an explanation that science has offered for the origin of life, and the unbelievable complexity of life, we are safe in the belief that there must be an ultimate cause for it all. There is an intelligent entity that does not require another cause. There is a genuine God.

Finally, there is another enormous reason why beings like the engineers could never suffice: the afterlife. Ever since I truly began to consider the issue of the afterlife in the context of the ancient astronaut perspective, I have been both perplexed and saddened by it. To illustrate the problem, consider something that was offered in Erich Von Däniken's book, *Evidence of the Gods* (which I found to be very interesting). At one point, he tells of a creation story that comes from the native peoples of the island chain of Kiribati, in the Pacific Ocean. They tell of a story about the god Nareau. Nareau is believed to be the creator of our world, and everything in it.

In this, there are unmistakable similarities between what Nareau is believed to have done and what the Bible says God did. Both are generally believed to have separated heaven from earth (vaguely, in Nareau's case), created plants, animals, and human beings in that order, and several other things. These are not small points, but it is the differences between Nareau and Yahweh that are important at present. You see, Nareau is a space traveler.[197] He is an "ancient astronaut" in the truest sense of the term.

While sleeping on his "interstellar spaceship," as Von Däniken explained it, he heard his name being called (by whom?). When he awoke, he looked down and saw Te Bomatemaki: earth and sky together. After landing his spacecraft (on Earth), he essentially finds it suitable for habitation. He seeds plants, creates animals, and then creates human beings. His purposes in creating life on this planet were very clear: "The space travelers must survive, replenish their food stocks. That requires food and drink—organic material."[198]

We were not made for Nareau's good pleasure, or for our own; we were made so Nareau could harvest our supplies when (and if) need be. Von Däniken also notes the "important addition" that ethnologist Arthur Grimble made to this story: "And when the work was done, Nareau, the creator, said: 'Enough! It has been done! I go, never to return!' So he went, never to return, and no one knows where he has been since then."[199] Not only was humanity a potential means to a nutritional end, Nareau had

---

[197] See *Evidence of the Gods*, 24-28, for the detailed account of Nareau. As an aside, I highly recommend reading the entire book, because it is both fascinating and highly informative.
[198] Ibid. 27
[199] Ibid.

no use for us otherwise. Maybe we would hear from him again, and maybe we would not.

In the ancient astronaut view, both Nareau and the engineers of *Prometheus* are exactly the types of entities that were there "in the beginning" of our story. Essentially, an extraterrestrial intelligence somehow arose elsewhere in the universe—how does a being (Nareau) who lives inside of the universe also create it?—came across our specific area, and seeded life on our planet. But the first part is the most important one, at present. If the being/s who created us are nothing more than older versions of us, how could they perform a miracle like raising the dead and bringing us back to life? As I mentioned concerning Jesus' miracles, this would require a metaphysical, otherworldly power; it is not simply a matter of scientific discovery.

But let's grant that these extraterrestrials could ultimately discover many secrets of biology and medicine beyond our scope of understanding, and that they were able to bring long-deceased individuals back to life. There are nearly eight billion people alive today, and billions of others have perished throughout history. What about all of us, all of them, and all who will be?

Having more sophisticated technology is one thing, but having an unimaginably detailed knowledge of billions of people's lives—which would be necessary in order to judge them, or to determine their quality—is another. Bringing a person back from the dead is one thing, but bringing billions of people back would be something very different. Again, it is not about technological advancement, but about extraordinary power! When it comes to the issue of the afterlife, the ancient astronaut view feels extremely bleak and desolate. Extraterrestrials from another planet created us, and intervened in our history at certain times (mostly long ago), but are completely impotent to help us against our greatest foe—death. More than that, it is questionable if they care about us at all. As in the Nareau legend: "I go, never to return!"

What would be the point? How could we have hope beyond this life, and why should we care about a creator who functionally has nothing to do with us individually? Some being flew over the Earth, found it habitable, created us, and then left, leaving no indication that it would come back for us. On a personal level, so what? Even if something like the engineers did create us, they would not be worthy of our worship or adoration. Neither would Nareau. *But Yahweh would.* They could not ultimately help us to live again, but *He could.* Moreover, they don't even appear to have an interest in doing so; our well-being is not a priority, and that is putting it mildly.

As I have described in previous sections of the book, Yahweh is not that kind of deity. This can be seen all throughout the Bible, from Yahweh's efforts in the Old Testament, to Jesus' extraordinary feats in the New Testament. God has power over life, death, sickness, and whatever else that really matters. Along with that, God cares about these things, and about each of us. Further, we also know about our future. Since Christ rose from the dead, so shall we. We have the promise of the resurrection, and the knowledge that Jesus will indeed return. God has not left us, or abandoned us. He is no "engineer," or even a Nareau; we know where things stand with Yahweh. What an indescribable difference!

This brings us to the last major point within the book, which I have at least touched on already in this closing section. The extraterrestrial presence we see in our world and in history could very well be more advanced beings like us, who just happened to arise on some other planet in the universe. Issues like the construction of otherwise impossible architecture, the seeding of life on Earth, and certain others, could be explained by these types of visitors. Those from the ancient astronaut background certainly believe this is the best explanation. While we cannot exclude the possibility that other beings exist elsewhere in the universe—that there are "aliens," in the most commonly understood sense of the word—we have not found definitive proof of their existence in all of our searching. We have not explored our entire universe (and we never will), but based on what we have seen thus far, no one else is out there.

Beyond that fact, I do not believe these types of beings could account for everything we see, in principle. The problem of having to explain the origin of life would apply to them, just as it does to us. If it took intelligence to spawn us, then it took intelligence to spawn them, too. The formation of life was so probable that it actually happened, but so improbable that it only happened once. That conundrum can never be eliminated, regardless of how many alien beings we place before us.

This compounds with all the other issues I have mentioned about beings who have to fly across the universe, just to get to our world. Issues like demonic possession and spontaneous human combustion require an unseen power, not one that flew across space in an aircraft. Never mind the previous point that power, not technology, is what would be required to raise every person from the dead, create numbers and install them into the fabric of our existence, control the weather, and many other things. As Willy Wonka said, "candy is dandy, but liquor is quicker." Technology is great, but power is essential.

It is true that angelic beings have crafts— "chariots," if you will— but they can also appear to us in a flash because there is no separation between our world and theirs. The heavenly kingdom is not in the sky, but is a realm that lies overtop of our own. As I have shown throughout the book, and in great detail elsewhere,[200] this is exactly how the Bible really describes things. Jesus showed this ability, and so did the angels all throughout the Bible. They appeared, disappeared, and sometimes reappeared, in an instant. They pass seamlessly between our realm and their own (heaven). If the ancient astronaut theorists want to start talking about beings from another dimension, or something of the sort, then their views will merge even closer with the biblical one. Some already have, to their credit.[201] That, however, is a tacit admission that beings who live

---

[200] See *The Death Myth,* 89-100, for a detailed explanation of how heaven is not in the sky, but is a different realm of existence altogether.

elsewhere within the universe cannot account for all of the activity we have seen in our world.

In closing, I leave you with a few thoughts to consider. The universe we inhabit is full of mystery, and there are many questions for which we will probably never have satisfying answers. More incredible things have happened on our own tiny planet than we will ever know about, much less be able to fully comprehend. But the search for truth and understanding continues, and it always should. With all of the things we are yet to grasp hold of, I believe we can rest assured of two critical realities about existence.

The first is that there are indeed beings—of both the good and evil varieties—of higher power and intelligence that survey our world and, at times, intervene in it. We see them riding in flying vehicles, in the advanced architecture of the ancient world, within our most prominent religious traditions, and especially through history's greatest texts. The second, and most unassailable, truth about reality is this: whatever beings we may encounter, wherever that may occur, and however it may happen, God remains the necessary and ultimate cause of all life. God made us . . . and He made the aliens too.

If you enjoyed this book, you can keep up with my blogs and other works at https://angels-aliens.com/. Thank you for reading, and God bless.

---

[201] I think of Philip Coppens, in particular. He feels very comfortable talking about the idea that extraterrestrials might actually be from a different dimension, rather than just a different planet. I suggest reading *The Ancient Alien Question*, where this view is quite prevalent.

REFERENCES

All Bible quotations are from the New American Standard Bible (NASB), unless otherwise noted.

Adl-Tabatabai, Sean. "1890 NY Times Article: Race of Giants Discovered in NewYork."YourNewsWire.Mar5,2018.

https://yournewswire.com/nytimes-race-giants-new-york/

Allconnect. "Why We Use 7 Digits and Other Fun Phone Facts." May 2, 2016. https://www.allconnect.com/blog/why-we-use-7-digits-and-other-fun-facts/

Al-Serri, Hamed. "The Great Pyramid Mystery Solved." National Geographic. YouTube. https://www.youtube.com/watch?v=Ws4O5LOCI68

Ammi, Ken. "On the giant of Castelnau." TrueFreeThinker. http://www.truefreethinker.com/articles/giant-castelnau

"Ancient Engineering mysteries: How did Ancient Mankind move and cut mega-lithic blocks of stone?" Ancient Code. https://www.ancient-code.com/ancient-engineering-mysteries-how-did-ancient-mankind-move-and-cut-megalithic-blocks-of-stone/

"Ancient Pyramids Match the Alignment of Orion's Belt." June 10. 2013. https://coolinterestingstuff.com/ancient-pyramids-match-the-alignment-of-orions-belt

Anthony, Sebastian. "Harvard cracks DNA storage, crams 700 terabytes of data into a singlegram".ExtremeTech.17August,2012. https://www.extremetech.com/extreme/134672-harvard-cracks-dna-storage-crams-700-terabytes-of-data-into-a-single-gram]

Asis, Adrian. "6 Cases of 'Demonic Possession' That Might Convince You". The Richest. 2 April, 2014.
http://www.therichest.com/rich-list/most-shocking/6-cases-of-demonic-possession-that-might-convince-you/

Robert Ballard, "Ballard and the Black Sea". National Geographic. http://www.nationalgeographic.com/blacksea/ax/frame.html

Barclay, Shelly. "The Better and Barney Hill Abduction." Historic Mysteries. Aug. 1, 2013. https://www.historicmysteries.com/betty-and-barney-hill-abduction/

TheBookofEnoch,chapterCVI,vv.5-6.

http://www.sacred-texts.com/bib/boe/boe110.htm

BensonCommentary."1Samuel17:4."

BibleHubCommentaries.http://biblehub.com/commentaries/1_samuel/17-4.htm

Bocchino, Peter. Geisler, Norman. Unshakeable Foundations. Bethany House Pub-lishers. Minneapolis, MN. 2001.

Booth, Billy. "Best Cases of Alien Abduction." ThoughtCo. Dec. 21, 2017. https://www.thoughtco.com/best-cases-of-alien-abduction-3293341

Browne, Malcolm W. "Whale Fossils High in Andes Show How Mountains Rose from Sea." The New York Times. 1987. https://www.nytimes.com/1987/03/12/us/whale-fossils-high-in-andes-show-how-mountains-rose-from-sea.html

Burchell, M.J. "Panspermia today". International Journal of Astrobiology. 24 December 2004.

https://www.cambridge.org/core/journals/international-journal-of-astrobiology/article/panspermia-today/6BD35AABC8832E4990AAA704B867489F

"Can DNA Prove the Existence of an Intelligent Designer?" Biola Magazine, 2010. http://magazine.biola.edu/article/10-summer/can-dna-prove-the-existence-of-an-intelligent-desi/

Colavito, Jason. "Ancient Astronaut Hypocrisy: Did Erich von Daniken Think Jesus Was an Astronaut?" Sept. 15, 2012.

http://www.jasoncolavito.com/blog/ancient-astronaut-hypocrisy-did-erich-von-daniken-think-jesus-was-an-astronaut

Coppens, Phillip. The Ancient Alien Question: A New Inquiry Into the Existence, Evidence, and Influence of Ancient Visitors. New Page Books. Pompton Plains, NJ. 2012, Print.

Corliss, William R., Mysteries Beneath the Sea, Apollo Editions, June 1975.

CE4 Research Group. "Quotes." http://www.alienresistance.org/ce4quotes.htm

"Cradle of Civilization." Wikipedia. https://en.wikipedia.org/wiki/Cradle_of_civilization

David, C. "The most legit UFO sightings." Grunge. http://www.grunge.com/9290/legit-ufo-sightings/

Davies, Paul. The Fifth Miracle: The Search for the Origin and Meaning of Life. Simon & Schuster, New York, NY. 1999. Print.

Dawkins, Richard. The God Delusion, Great Britain: Bantam Press, 2006. Print.

Dell'Amore, Christine. "Ancient Roman Giant Found—Oldest Complete Skele-ton WithGigantism."NationalGeographic.Nov10,2012.

https://news.nationalgeographic.com/news/2012/11/121102-gigantism-ancient-skeleton-archaeology-history-science-rome/

"Desert whale graveyard mystery solved: Fossils of 40 whales, along with seals, dolphins and aquatic sloths found at site." CBC News. Feb 27, 2014. http://www.cbc.ca/news/technology/desert-whale-graveyard-mystery-solved-1.2554045

"Devils and Demons". Mythencyclopedia.com. http://www.mythencyclopedia.com/Cr-Dr/Devils-and-Demons.html

Devlin, Hannah. "No single birthplace of mankind, say scientists." The Guardian. Jul 11, 2018.

https://www.theguardian.com/science/2018/jul/11/no-single-birthplace-of-mankind-say-scientists

"Drain the Oceans: Legends of Atlantis" (S5E1). National Geographic. https://www.nationalgeographic.com/tv/watch/6a6e48bf50630f9f6d6a8e71cfde7704/

Duchesne-Guillemin, Jacques. "Zoroastrianism." Encyclopaedia Britannica. https://www.britannica.com/topic/Zoroastrianism

Ehrman, Bart D. God's Problem: How the Bible Fails to Answer Our Most Important Question—Why We Suffer. HarperOne. New York, NY. 2008, Print.

Enuma Elish: Epic of Creation. L.W. King Translator. http://www.sacred-texts.com/ane/enuma.htm

Evarts, Ben. "Spontaneous combustion or chemical reaction". NFPA. Nov, 2011. http://www.nfpa.org/news-and-research/fire-statistics-and-reports/fire-statistics/fire-causes/chemical-and-gases/spontaneous-combustion-or-chemical-reaction

Fairfield, Hannah. "Finding Noah's Flood: Evidence of Ancient Disaster Is LinkedtoBiblicalLegend".ColumbiaNews.Nov19,1999. http://www.columbia.edu/cu/news/99/11/flood.html

Fairfield, Hannah, "Noah's Flood: Evidence of Ancient Disaster Is Linked to Bib-lical Legend". Columbia University Record. Vol. 24, No. 12. Jan 21, 1999. http://www.columbia.edu/cu/news/99/11/flood.html

"Floods". Myths Encyclopedia. http://www.mythencyclopedia.com/Fi-Go/Floods.html

Fredericksen,Linwood."AngelandDemon".EncyclopaediaBritannica. https://www.britannica.com/topic/angel-religion

Fuchs, Shair; Milo, Ron; Sender, Ron. "Revised Estimates for the Number of HumanandBacteriaCellsintheBody."PlosBiology.Aug19,2016. http://journals.plos.org/plosbiology/article?id=10.1371/journal.pbio.1002533#sec002

Gannon, Megan. "Study: the First Americans Didn't Arrive by the Bering Land Bridge."MentalFloss.Aug10,2016.

http://mentalfloss.com/article/84506/first-americans-didnt-arrive-bering-land-bridge-study-says

Gates, Bill. The Road Ahead. Penguin Press. London, England. Print. 1996.

"Giants of Other Days: Recent Discoveries Near Serpent Mound, Ohio." The New York Times. Mar 5, 1894.

https://timesmachine.nytimes.com/timesmachine/1894/03/05/106899120.pdf

Graham, Billy. "Did God Create Aliens." June 1, 2004. https://billygraham.org/answer/if-there-is-intelligent-life-on-other-planets-does-god-care-about-those-creatures-as-much-as-he-does-us/

Handley, Andrew. "Top 10 Unsolved Cases of Spontaneous Human Combus-tion". TopTenz. Dec. 12, 2011. http://www.toptenz.net/top-10-unsolved-cases-of-spontaneous-human-combustion.php

Hara, Tetsuya, Kajiura, Daigo Takagi, Kazuma. "Transfer of Life-Bearing Meteor-ites from Earth to Other Planets". Journal of Cosmology. 8 Apr 2012. https://arxiv.org/abs/1204.1719

HealthResearchFunding.org. "16 Interesting Gigantism Statistics." Nov. 28, 2014. https://healthresearchfunding.org/16-interesting-gigantism-statistics/

Hilkevitch, Jon. "In the sky! A bird? A plane? A . . . UFO?" Chicago Tribune. Jan 01, 2007. http://articles.chicagotribune.com/2007-01-01/travel/chi-0701010141jan01_1_craig-burzych-controllers-in-o-hare-tower-united-plane

History Staff. "Is spontaneous human combustion real?" History. Feb. 6, 2013. http://www.history.com/news/ask-history/is-spontaneous-human-combustion-real

Hodge, Bodie. "Who Were the Nephilim: Genesis 6 and Numbers 13—a Fresh

Look." AnswersinGenesis.Jul9,2008.https://answersingenesis.org/bible-characters/who-were-the-nephilim/

Holloway, April. "Gun-Yu and the Chinese Flood Myth." http://www.ancient-origins.net/myths-legends/gun-yu-and-chinese-flood-myth-00370

Horgan, John. "In the Beginning." Scientific American, pg. 120. February, 1991.

"How much of the ocean have we explored?" National Ocean Service. Oct. 10, 2017.
https://oceanservice.noaa.gov/facts/exploration.html

Howe, Tom. "A Reponse to Bart D. Ehrman's Misquoting Jesus." http://www.isca-apologetics.org/papers/isca-2006/response-bart-d-ehrmans-misquoting-jesus

"Human Combustion Victim." Science Channel. http://www.sciencechannel.com/tv-shows/the-unexplained-files/videos/spontaneous-combustion-victim/

Owen Jarus, "How Were the Egyptian Pyramids Built?" LiveScience. Jun 14, 2016. https://www.livescience.com/32616-how-were-the-egyptian-pyramids-built-.html

Kean, Leslie.UFOs: Generals, Pilots, and Government Officials Go on the Record. Harmony Books. New York, NY. 2010.

Klein, Christopher, "DNA Study Finds Aboriginal Australians World's Oldest Civilization." History. September, 2016. http://www.history.com/news/dna-study-finds-aboriginal-australians-worlds-oldest-civilization

Kiger, Patrick J. "Australian Aboriginal Creation Stories." National Geographic. http://channel.nationalgeographic.com/the-story-of-god-with-morgan-freeman/articles/australian-aboriginal-creation-stories/

Kiger, Patrick J. "Top 10 Mass Sightings of UFOs." National Geographic. June 11, 2012.http://channel.nationalgeographic.com/chasing-ufos/articles/top-10-mass-sightings-of-ufos/

Kim, Michelle. "How Cremation Works". Howstuffworks. http://science.howstuffworks.com/cremation1.htm

Kluger, Jeffrey. "Here's Proof That the First Modern Humans Were Chinese." Time. Oct 14, 2015. http://time.com/4071342/earliest-humans-china/

Krystek, Lee. "Khufu's Great Pyramid." http://www.unmuseum.org/kpyramid.htm

Kramer, Samuel Noah. History Begins at Sumer. Garden City, N.Y.: Doubleday / Anchor, 1959.

Marks, Joshua J. "Enuma Elish - The Babylonian Epic of Creation." March 2, 2011. http://www.ancient.eu/article/225/

"Mayan Scientific Achievements." History.com. https://www.history.com/topics/mayan-scientific-achievements

McCoy, Dan, "Ginnungagap." Norse Mythology for Smart People. http://norse-mythology.org/cosmology/ginnungagap/

Morris, Henry M. The Genesis Record: A Scientific and Devotional Commentary on the Book of Beginnings. Baker Book House. Grand Rapids, MI. 1976.

Padula, Richard. "The day UFOs stopped play." BBC News. Oct. 24, 2014. http://www.bbc.com/news/magazine-29342407

"Panspermia: Transfer of Life Between Stars, Galaxies & Planets". Journal of Cos-mology. http://journalofcosmology.com/Contents7.html

Little, Greg. "The truth about giant skeletons in American Indian mounds, and theSmithsoniancover-up."APMagazine.Jun.2014.SecretHistory. https://www.sott.net/article/281093-The-truth-about-giant-skeletons-in-American-Indian-mounds-and-the-Smithsonian-cover-up

Lovgren, Stefan. "Who Were the First Americans?" National Geographic News. Sept3,2003.

http://news.nationalgeographic.com/news/2003/09/0903_030903_bajaskull.html

McClellan, Jason. "Spiders blamed for mass UFO sighting." Open Minds. Oct 24, 2014.http://www.openminds.tv/spiders-blamed-mass-ufo-sighting/30736

McDowell, Josh. "What are the Dead Sea Scrolls and Why Do They Matter?" Jan. 6, 2016. http://seanmcdowell.org/blog/what-are-the-dead-sea-scrolls-and-why-do-they-matter

Mohamadi, A.l.i., Salvatori, Roberto. Handbook of Neuroendocrinology, "Neuroendo-crine Growth Disorders – Dwarfism, Gigantism." 2012. ScienceDirect. https://www.sciencedirect.com/topics/neuroscience/gigantism

Moye, David. "Frank Baker Discusses Spontaneous Combustion Experience On 'The UnexplainedFiles'."Huffpost.Oct.1,2013.

http://www.huffingtonpost.com/2013/10/01/frank-baker-spontaneous-combustion_n_4024833.html

Ohio History Connection. "Serpent Mound." https://www.ohiohistory.org/visit/museum-and-site-locator/serpent-mound

Osborne, Hannah. "Ancient Egyptian Pharaoh is World's Oldest Case of Gigan-tism." Newsweek. Aug. 7, 2017. http://www.newsweek.com/ancient-egypt-giant-pharaoh-king-sanakht-647292

Oskin, Becky. "Incredible Technology: How to Track Hurricanes". Live Science. Sept 16, 2013.http://www.livescience.com/39678-incredible-tech-track-hurricanes.html

Petersen, Mikkel W. (et al.) "Postglacial viability and colonization in North Ameri-ca's ice-free corridor." Nature. Aug 10, 2016. https://www.nature.com/articles/nature19085

Plubins, Rodrigo Quijada. "Chariot." The Ancient History Encyclopedia. March 6, 2013. https://www.ancient.eu/chariot/

"Project Phoenix." The SETI Institute. https://seti.org/

"Pyramids of Giza." Encyclopaedia Britannica. https://www.britannica.com/topic/Pyramids-of-Giza

Rammel,E.C. "Pangu and the Chinese Creation." Story- http://www.ancient-origins.net/human-origins-folklore/pangu-and-chinese-creation-myth-00347

Robinson, Maurice A. "The Integrity of the Early New Testament Text: A Colla-tion-Based Comparison Utilizing the Papyri of the Second and Third Centuries" (Valley Forge, Pennsylvania: Evangelical Theological Society: 57th Annual Meeting, 2005), 3-4.

"RoboticMarsExploration."NASA.gov.

https://www.nasa.gov/mission_pages/mars/images/index.html

Rossiter, Brian. The Death Myth: Uncovering What the Bible Really Says about the Afterlife. pg. 136. iUniverse. Bloomington, IN. Copyright, 2018. Print.

Rossiter, Brian M., Wayne D. Mind Over Matter: The Necessity of Metaphysics in a Material World. Athanatos Publishing Group. 2016. Print.

Wiliam, Ryan. "Status of the Black Sea Hypothesis." Columbia University.January,2007.

https://www.researchgate.net/publication/265937032_Status_of_the_Black_Sea_flood_hypothesis

Sample, Ian. "Fossil sperm whale with huge teeth found in Peruvian desert." The Guardian.Jun30,2010.

https://www.theguardian.com/science/2010/jun/30/fossil-sperm-whale-huge-teeth

Schenkman, Lauren. "In the Brian, Seven Is A Magic Number." ABC News. Dec.6,2009.https://abcnews.go.com/Technology/brain-memory-magic-number/story?id=9189664

"SETI Research." The SETI Institute. https://seti.org/

"SpaceExploration."EncyclopaediaBritannica,https://www.britannica.com/science/space-exploration/Major-milestones.

Snyder, Christopher. "Did the story of Noah really happen?" Fox News. Mar 28, 2014.
http://www.foxnews.com/science/2014/03/28/did-story-noah-really-happen.html

"TheCreation."

http://www.greekmythology.com/Myths/The_Myths/The_Creation/the_creation.html

"TheEpicofGilgamesh."Tablet1.AncientTexts.

http://www.ancienttexts.org/library/mesopotamian/gilgamesh/tab1.htm

Slick, Matt. "Manuscript evidence for superior New Testament reliability." CARM.org. Dec. 10, 2008. https://carm.org/manuscript-evidence

Smith'sBibleDictionary,"Horse."

https://www.biblestudytools.com/dictionary/horse/

Smith, Trey. "Nephilim: True Story of Satan, Fallen Angels, Giants, Aliens, Hy-brids,Elongatedskulls&Nephilim."Aug.21,2013. https://www.youtube.com/watch?v=1zz8_MxcnzY&t=687s

Speigel, Lee. "UFO-Alien Abduction Still Haunts Travis Walton." Weird News. https://www.huffingtonpost.com/2015/04/23/travis-walton-still-haunted-by-ufo_n_7119910.html

"Sumerian Myth." http://faculty.gvsu.edu/websterm/SumerianMyth.htm

The Washington Post, "The self-possessed psychiatrist Richard Gallagher should exorcisehisdelu-sions."July15,2016.https://www.washingtonpost.com/opinions/this-self-possessed-psychiatrist-should-exorcise-his-delusions/2016/07/15/556b78e2-4877-11e6-8dac-

0c6e4accc5b1_story.html?noredirect=on&utm_term=.fb317a9729a0

Tomkins, Jeffrey P. "Bewildering Pseudogene Functions Both Forwards and Backwards." Institute of Creation Research. Jun 14, 2013. http://www.icr.org/article/7542/

Tsoulakos, Giorgio. "Aliens and Sacred Places." Ancient Aliens. S3E3.

Vallee, Jacques. Messengers of Deception: UFO Contacts and Cults. Daily Grail Publish-ing, Am. Edition. June 1, 2008.

"Victory Stele of Naram-Sin." Department of Near Eastern Antiquities: Mesopo-tamia. The Louvre. https://www.louvre.fr/en/oeuvre-notices/victory-stele-naram-sin

Vintini, Leonardo. "Noah's Ark and the Great Flood, Did it Really Happen?" TheEpochTimes.May18,2013. https://www.theepochtimes.com/was-there-really-a-great-flood_61371.html?

Von Däniken, Erich. Evidence of the Gods: A Visual Tour of Alien Influence in the Ancient World. Career Press. Pompton Plains, NJ. 2013. Print.

Wald, George. "The Origin of Life," Scientific American, 191:45-53, Aug 1954.

Warnock, Christopher. "Hermes Trismegistus: Hermetic Philosophy, Astrology &Magic."http://www.renaissanceastrology.com/hermestrismegistus.html

Waterlow, Lucy. "Aliens want to steal my soul: British woman claims she's been repeatedly abducted by 'reptilian' extraterrestrials."

Dailymail. April, 2014. http://www.dailymail.co.uk/femail/article-2614899/Aliens-want-steal-soul-British-woman-reveals-shes-abducted-reptilian-extraterrestrials-numerous-occasions.html

"What is Gigantism?" Healthline. https://www.healthline.com/health/gigantism

"What are the odds of a dead dinosaur becoming fossilized?" Scientific American. Sep 16, 2002.https://www.scientificamerican.com/article/what-are-the-odds-of-a-de/

Wikipedia. "7." Accessed May 23, 2018. https://en.wikipedia.org/wiki/7

"Yonaguni Pyramid." The Faram Research Foundation. http://www.yonaguni.ws/

Made in the USA
Columbia, SC
06 January 2023

75736259R00104